SPEAK LIKE A LEADER
Zing!

"I know great speakers are not born but decide to be made. This book is a great resource for those who've decided to become great speakers."
Diane Smith-Gander
President, Chief Executive Women and well-respected non-executive Director

"If you have ever thought of becoming a professional speaker or you struggle with speaking in front of people then this book will be perfect for you. Mark explains things expertly for any reader and as someone who speaks at over 100 conferences each year, it made perfect sense to me and reminded me of some areas I too had to address when starting out."
Justin Herald
Managing Director, Major Motivation
and author, *Would you like Attitude with that?*

"Zing! Speak Like A Leader converts complex concepts into well structured and easy-to-implement actions that will unlock your potential as an engaging and influential speaker. Insightful, refreshingly practical and down to earth this rich speaking resource will help any speaker, from new leader through to seasoned professional, to better inform, entertain and inspire their audience".
Ian Hutchinson
Founder, LifebyDesign.com.au
and Professional Speakers Australia Hall of Fame,
Educator of the Year

"Having fallen into the field of public speaking due to my career in cricket, I wish this book has been available at the time to assist me. Not only does the author address all aspects of becoming a confident speaker, he also provides real life examples, which make it very readable. It doesn't matter if you hate public speaking or enjoy it, Mark addresses all levels and provides some handy hints along the way."

Lisa Sthalekar

Former International Cricketer

To my parents, Enid and Vincent,
for all your love and support.

Also to my children, Kimberley and Joshua,
that you may gain inspiration from these pages.

Author's note: All personal examples in this book are factual. However, in some cases, names have been intentionally changed to protect the privacy of individuals.

Copyright © Mark D'Silva 2016

The moral right of the author has been asserted.

National Library of Australia Cataloguing-in-Publication entry has been applied for.

978-0-9953857-0-2 Print-on-Demand (IngramSpark)
978-0-9953857-1-9 ePub
978-0-9953857-2-6 mobi
978-0-9953857-3-3 Traditional Print
978-0-9953857-4-0 CreateSpace

Custom book production by Captain Honey
Cover and internal design by Natalie Winter
www.captainhoney.com.au

5 4 3 2 1   16 17 18 19 20

SPEAK LIKE A LEADER

Zing!

MARK D'SILVA

Contents

Foreword

I am delighted to write the foreword for this magnificent book *Zing! Speak Like A Leader*, particularly because the book has the potential to change so many lives for the better.

I enjoy the distinction of being the first person from outside North America to win the prestigious 'Toastmasters International World Championship Of Public Speaking'. Such a win substantially changed my life in ways unimaginable prior to that occasion.

I recall reading a truism that while great oratory can rightly be considered to be an art, public speaking can be considered to be a craft. I have come to the conclusion that a major purpose of this book is to help its readers become competent at the craft of public speaking by providing them with easy-to-use activities and strategies in order to develop the necessary competencies. 'Zing! Speak Like A Leader' is also designed to help readers on their journey to becoming leaders and speaking like leaders. The practice of these competencies will, no doubt over time, lead to life changing outcomes.

I have known the author of this book, Mark D'Silva, for many years and can endorse that he is a highly qualified practitioner of the public speaking craft. He has delivered countless presentations, been a NSW public speaking champion on 3 occasions and has run numerous workshops on the subject.

As a person Mark possesses the outstanding human quality of genuineness. Genuineness is widely acknowledged as an essential ingredient in communicating with sincerity.

Not one to rest on his laurels, Mark is continually in pursuit of further personal growth and self-development as he ascribes to the philosophy that the more knowledge he gains, the more he can help others.

I have no doubt that the reader's investment of time and effort in the practice of the activities and strategies recommended in this book, will lead to outstanding and worthy rewards.

Ken Bernard
World Champion of Public Speaking,
Toastmasters International

Introduction

Imagine you have come to a fork in the road. There are two paths at this juncture. One path is called the *Uninspired Speakers* path. The other is called the *Outstanding Speakers* path. Let's look at each path.

The Uninspired Speakers Path

Some people decide to take the *Uninspired Speakers* path. If you travel down this path, you may be a speaker who is fearful each time you are asked to present. Perhaps you are not convinced you have a message valuable enough to share, so you are constantly filled with self-doubt.

'What will my audience think?'

'What if they don't understand me?'

'What if I fail?'

Without even realising it, if you are this type of speaker you are focusing on yourself more than on the audience. If you do not know how to connect with the audience, it's likely you'll have nagging doubts about your presenting ability and concerns about what can go wrong. This self-doubt may be due to lack of knowledge or understanding of how to clearly structure your messages. Fear may mask your natural charm and good sense of humour, and a lack of self-esteem relegate you to the position of follower rather than leader.

Imagine this. At the end of the Uninspired Speakers path is a house; it is the speaker's residence. It is a modest house with only one door. The door to *limited opportunities*. Even though the speaker works hard, takes pride in what they do, has admirable values and is a good person, they only have the basics: a basic house, basic furniture, a basic life. Their inability to communicate well has inhibited progress. This has resulted in deteriorating relationships, fewer job promotion opportunities and diminished success in life.

MY STORY

I know the Uninspired Speakers path very well. *Intimately, in fact.* Because that is the path I chose many years ago. *Chose* is probably not the right word. *Settled for* is a better phrase. Yes, I settled for the *Uninspired Speakers* path.

Don't get me wrong. I *wanted* to succeed. I had a great work ethic. I had good values and ambitions to climb the corporate ladder.

One thing kept *blocking* that step-up to the next rung on the ladder. *Poor communication skills.*

Yes, I considered myself an ineffective communicator. This led to many frustrations with my family, friends and work colleagues. The inability to get my message across simply and easily made me feel demoralised. This resulted in unhappiness, insecurity and low self-esteem.

I clearly remember at one annual performance appraisal at work, my manager discussed some of the communication challenges I was facing. She suggested a course of action. She gave me the responsibility of presenting to senior management each week. *Yikes!* Imagine my fear. All sorts of self-doubt plagued my mind. I kept asking myself:

'What if I fail?'
(Good odds)

'What if I retch in front my audience?'
(Possible)

'What if I can't remember what to say next?'
(That's happened to me before)

'What if the audience laughs at my inept presentation?'
(Great odds)

And on and on it went. There was only one person making me feel sick. *Me!*

I remember sneaking into the work locker room two hours prior to each weekly presentation to deal with my nerves and rehearse the best way that I could. And each week, without fail, I would do the same thing.

I would present with my heart pounding relentlessly. I was sure that everyone in the room could hear every throbbing beat. I constantly stumbled over words as I rushed to complete the presentation to get it over and done with. And I silently prayed that no-one would ask questions. Of course, Murphy's Law was always present and the audience would ask questions. So, I would try to answer, and once again I stuttered, stumbled and mumbled another incoherent, nonsensical reply.

On one occasion, I asked a work colleague who was also a good friend to attend the meeting and critique me. After the meeting, he gave it to me straight. 'Don't take this personally, but you were crap.' Did I mention that he was a friend? At least he was honest. But that one comment really hit home … hard!

That night was a sleepless one as I reflected on my options.

Did I want to continue down the Uninspired Speakers path?

Did I want to live with deteriorating relationships at home, at work and at play?

Did I want to settle for little success and a modest life?

The answers were clear. A resounding No! Enough was enough. The pain had become unbearable. *There is no more powerful motivator than pain.* Psychologists say that most people will only change if they perceive the pain to be excruciating. For me the pain of ineffective communication and pathetic presenting was excruciating.

So, I made a decision. A tough decision. A decision that required me to muster all my courage.

I decided not to settle for the *Uninspired Speakers* way of life. I decided to leave the comfort of the modest house. I decided to walk back down the path of the Uninspired Speakers and head towards the fork in the road.

Over the next few months I joined a public speaking organisation and actively participated in workshops and events that increased my speaking skills. My journey towards becoming a better speaker had begun.

The Outstanding Speakers Path

Now let's look at the Outstanding Speakers path. If you travel down this path, you are a confident presenter, secure in your speaking abilities and possessing strong self-esteem. Your communication is clear and succinct. Those who communicate with you always *get* what you're saying. You communicate your ideas in a compelling way with a comprehensible and strong benefit for the intended audience. Each time you present, it is with a clear sense of purpose. Your message is structured and logical.

You connect really well with people; it's because you care for them and are respectful of their feelings. People always say great things about you.

'He really knows how to inspire an audience.'

'He knows exactly what issues bug us and provides clear and workable actions to resolve them.'

'He has a wonderful sense of humour and connects with his powerful, uplifting stories.'

You are passionate in everything that you do. This has a positive impact on the people around you who are vitalised by your infectious energy.

As an outstanding speaker, you have the x-factor that most people crave. It's called charisma.

You also have great leadership qualities. People look up to you as a role model and are motivated by your message to take positive action.

As you head up the Outstanding Speakers path you come to your house. It's a grand mansion, adorned by wonderful lush gardens, an inviting swimming pool and beautiful furnishings. There are many doors to your mansion representing *unlimited opportunities* that are opening up to you.

Your mansion reminds you of how far you have come and it is the result of your success. And most of it has been achieved through your ability to communicate, your flair in inspiring others, and your leadership capability.

Taking the path of the *Outstanding Speaker* represents success.

A NOTE ON THE TWO PATHS

Please note that even though I have used the analogy of houses, I am not implying that actually living in a modest house or a mansion is a measure of your success as a speaker or a person. The analogy is for illustrative purposes only. Rather, your goal for success should be to develop the personal qualities, skills and capabilities required to be a good speaker by learning and acting on the lessons and experiences outlined in this book.

Zing!

Why the book title 'Zing!'? Many years ago, during my Uninspired Speaker days, I had a generally apathetic outlook on life. Nothing would get me too excited and I certainly lacked energy. I clearly remember the day when my outlook changed.

I was working on an assignment with a project manager and we received a significant award at work, a terrific endorsement for a hugely successful delivery. I remember the project manager coming to my desk to share in the glory. He raised his hand for a high five and with great enthusiasm stated 'Wasn't that a fantastic achievement, Mark?'

I must have given him a muted response with a total lack of reciprocation for his enthusiasm. He turned to me and said 'Is that the best you can muster? C'mon Mark, put some zing into it.'

His reaction hit home. Later that evening as I reflected on his words, I realised that I was living life with little vigour and positive energy. My life lacked zing. From that moment I made a decision to live life with more zing.

If you want to be a great speaker, you need zing. Zing will add the x-factor that will draw audiences to you and guarantee speaking success.

Of course you also need other elements to build credibility and connect with your audience. Everything that you need is covered in this book and reading it will help to develop your speaking capabilities as you act on the ideas it contains.

Zing! is split into four dedicated parts:

- Confidence;

- Structure;

- Connect;

- Leadership.

Each part contains chapters designed to make you aware of what is required to become an outstanding speaker.

Part One: *Confidence*

Having confidence is the foundation of great public speaking. It means you know your own capabilities, and do not always take the safe ground. You begin to trust yourself, start doing things differently and taking calculated risks. This leads to small wins and greater confidence. Small wins turn into bigger wins and even greater self-confidence.

This part explores the challenges facing you if lack confidence and self-esteem. It outlines activities that will help you to live your life with confidence and secondly to use this assurance to become a great speaker.

Part Two: *Structure*

A clear purpose for your message and a logical structure are crucial elements in becoming a speaking success. Too often we see speakers who wing it and are unprepared for their speaking assignment.

The Structure part focuses on how to research, develop and organise your message quickly and easily. It also demonstrates how to grab your listeners' attention right from your opening statement, how to keep their attention through the body of your speech and how to close on a high.

Part Three: *Connect*

Great speakers have the ability to connect with their audience. They connect by creating anticipation. They connect through telling superb stories. They connect by using their unique sense of humour.

When they connect, they can sell their message. This part shows you how to connect with your audience using proven techniques that all great speakers use. Now you can use them too.

Part Four: *Leadership*

Outstanding speakers are confident. They are passionate. And above all, they are leaders. Leadership starts with taking charge of your life and then focusing on how you can help others make a difference to their lives.

The Leadership part outlines the leadership qualities that are essential to becoming an outstanding speaker. It demonstrates how to develop the leadership skills that may enable you to change your own life for the better and then help others.

How to Get the Most Out of this Book

You can read the book from cover to cover or go straight to the part that interests you. However, you will get the best out of this book by reading it cover to cover first, as there will be references to earlier chapters throughout the book.

ABOUT YOU

I recognise that speakers of different abilities will be reading this book, and I've designed it to work for all levels. Hopefully you should see yourself reflected in one of the categories below.

Novice Speakers

These speakers may never have presented or have had limited

speaking opportunities. The category may include people who have a very real fear of public speaking. They may want to find a way to get started with public speaking or simply develop their skills and confidence.

Intermediate Speakers

These speakers are more experienced than novice presenters. They may be looking for tips on how to increase their speaking effectiveness.

Advanced Speakers

These speakers are experienced and looking to add depth or that added edge to their public speaking.

FOR THE NOVICE SPEAKER

Reading this book is a courageous step on your journey to speak like a leader. I can assure you that you will never regret aspiring to become a better speaker.

Learn as much as you can from this book but more importantly, apply these techniques as soon as practicable. Procrastination is your mortal enemy, ready to block you as you move towards the Outstanding Speakers path. In fact, procrastination and apathy direct you towards the Uninspired Speakers path.

The Confidence part will be very useful to you, as will that on Structure, helping you to refine and position your message. Once you are comfortable with these two parts then continue with the rest of the journey.

I am your coach throughout this book and I hope that you can use the all of the ideas and strategies towards your future success.

FOR THE INTERMEDIATE SPEAKER

It's great that you want to continue on your journey towards becoming an outstanding speaker. You probably recognise that you already possess good speaking abilities and experience. You also know that there are skills that will enhance your capabilities.

While you may find that the first two parts, on Confidence and Structure, are useful, you may obtain more benefit from focusing on the Connection and Leadership parts, which will strongly support your journey towards mastery.

FOR THE ADVANCED SPEAKER

I am humbled that you are reading this book. It informs me that you are committed to life-long self-development.

The parts on Connection and Leadership will provide some useful tips and strategies, though you may also find some gems in the first two parts.

I wish you well on your journey and know that you will reach great heights as a speaker.

FOR ALL READERS

No matter what your speaking style or level of competency, I am sure that you will benefit from reading this book and applying the lessons. The book is a combination of strategies employed by great speakers worldwide and my own experiences obtained over the last 20 years as a speaker, trainer and coach.

About Me

For the first 30 years of my life, I considered myself shy and introverted. Growing up in Pakistan and being raised in a conservative Catholic family may have contributed to my risk-averse nature and low confidence.

In my early thirties I made a decision to become a leader. I sought out good leaders as mentors and embarked on self-development programs. Starting out as a trainee in the banking industry, I progressed to managing projects and leading teams and then established myself as a change management consultant. Doors continued to open for me. I accepted roles as president of a community organisation and on the boards of entrepreneurial organisations and established Speak 2 Peak with a mission to help people speak with confidence, sincerity and passion.

A Final Note

Mastering presentation skills is like mastering any other skill. First you need to know what to do. *Zing!* shows you how.

Next you need to apply in practice what you have learnt. This will be up to you. Make a commitment that you will use every opportunity to practise these strategies.

I am confident that these strategies will make you a better speaker and help on your journey to become an outstanding speaker.

I will be with you, in spirit, every step of the way and I wish you well on this exciting journey. Live your life with zing!

PART ONE
Confidence

Confidence is the foundation of speaking like a leader. For you to feel good about yourself and effectively connect with others, you need be cognisant of your fears, and know how to overcome them and build confidence.

This part of the book will introduce you to the concept of super-confidence versus arrogance and explore why fear is an obstacle to speaking success. We then look at strategies to help you build confidence and the secrets to learn from confident speakers. Here is an overview of the chapters in this part:

Super-Confidence

This chapter describes what super-confidence means and how it differs from arrogance. Here you will undertake an assessment of your own confidence level.

Why Fear is a Speaker's Nightmare

We discuss the two main fears humans are born with and how the flight-or-fight response affects us. This chapter sets the scene for becoming aware of what may be holding us back as speakers.

How to Build Confidence

We commence the process of building confidence. Learn how to effectively use affirmations and visualisation to build confidence. There are six more strategies that you can use every day to help improve your confidence levels.

Learn the Secrets of Confident Speakers

This chapter focuses on what confident speakers do to succeed. You will learn the importance of rehearsing your speech and remembering that the audience is on your side, how reading extensively can support you and, finally, an effective way to deal with anxiety.

CHAPTER 1

Super-Confidence

*'The brain is a wonderful thing. It starts the
moment you are born and never stops ...
until you get up to speak in public.'*

ANONYMOUS

Confidence may be described as a trust or belief that a course or action or thought is the correct one. Self-confidence means having the trust or belief in yourself that you can capably think through or do something.

Outstanding speakers have great self-confidence. They are comfortable with their chosen profession. They are confident in their interactions with all types of people. They are confident in their ability to present their message and influence their audience. Great speakers are so confident of their abilities, that one might say that they are super-confident.

Super-Confidence and Arrogance

Arrogance (or hubris) is considered as having confidence in

oneself that is unmerited. Someone who is arrogant may believe that they are capable or correct when they may not be. An arrogant person may also believe that they can do something better than others. They have 'tickets on themselves'. And they often want to tell others how good they are.

Do you know anyone who is *arrogant or egotistical?*
People who appear arrogant often actually suffer from low self-esteem. Arrogance may be a defence mechanism to help them cope with life. If they portray themselves as better than others, they feel good. Everyone wants to feel good. The arrogant person feels good by putting himself or herself *up* on a pedestal while putting others *down*.

THE DIFFERENCE BETWEEN CONFIDENT PEOPLE AND ARROGANT PEOPLE

Arrogant people are focused on *themselves*.
Confident people are focused on *other* people.

Arrogant people tend to *talk up* their success.
Confident people humbly *accept* their achievements and success.

Arrogant people often have *low* self-esteem.
Confident people have *high* self-esteem.

Arrogant people often want to be the *only* winner.
Confident people want *everyone* to be a winner.

Arrogant people are often selfish. It's me, me, me.
Confident people are unselfish. They are focused on helping others.

Outstanding speakers are not arrogant. They are confident. In fact they are super-confident.

What does Super-Confident Mean?

It means that the person is very comfortable with who they are. They understand their strengths and their weaknesses, play to their strengths and work hard to correct their weaknesses.

Super-confidence also means good self-esteem. These individuals are not overly sensitive to criticism. In fact, they welcome feedback as it provides the opportunity to see how others perceive them and thus to help them improve.

Outstanding speakers are super-confident in that they know the messages they convey will be of value to others.

The world today has some outstanding speakers who appear super-confident. US President Barack Obama is one such speaker. Confident when he is speaking to the US citizens, confident in his messages to the world media, and confident as he strives to manage relationships with the Middle East or North Korea. He always appears in total control and speaks in a measured, relaxed manner. *That is super-confidence.*

Do you know someone who is super-confident?

What makes them super-confident? Is it that they always have control over a situation? Is it because they are calm and relaxed when communicating with others? Is it due to their ability to communicate their message with clarity, simplicity and ease? Is it that they can influence others to take action? Or is it all of the above?

To me it is all of the above. So, let's now take a look at *you*.

Rate your Confidence Level

Try this self-assessment to get a gauge of your level of confidence as a presenter. For each statement, rate yourself from one to ten.

Rating yourself a one means that you strongly *agree* with the response.

Rating yourself a ten means that you strongly *disagree* with the statement.

SELF-ASSESSMENT STATEMENTS

- I find it difficult to get my message across in most circumstances.

- I often get frustrated when other people don't understand what I'm trying to say.

- I always let someone else lead the conversation.

- I find it difficult to speak impromptu with confidence.

- I feel extremely nervous and anxious prior to giving a presentation.

- I never structure my presentation because I don't know how.

- I worry that my presentation will end in disaster.

- I often feel unsure of the value I bring to my audience as a speaker.

- I get flustered when people ask me questions at my presentation.

- People often seem to lose interest halfway through my presentation.

Add up your scores from the self-assessment to see how you performed:

10 – 25   Your confidence levels are low. I can almost hear your heart thumping and feel your deep anxiety. But do not despair. This book will help. Read the part on Confidence a few times and apply as many strategies from it as you can. Think positively and know that your confidence will increase.

26 – 50   At the lower end of this scale you probably need to develop more self-confidence. At the higher end of this scale, you may have good communication skills but still get nervous and apprehensive when you have to present. The first two parts on Confidence and Structure provided in this book will certainly help.

51- 75   You are doing well, especially if you are at the higher end of this scale. You are more comfortable than most speakers and now need to get that extra edge. The Connection part will certainly help you to achieve this. You are well on your way.

76 – 100 You are already a confident communicator and speaker, so congratulations. You're almost there but possibly seeking those added extras that will lead you to become an outstanding speaker. The Care For Your Audience, Cultivate Charisma and Tell Stories chapters will be enormously beneficial. Just find those gems in this book that will work for you and test them out.

GET A SECOND OPINION

Now, here's a twist. Seek out a *trusted* person. This may be your partner, close friend or even a mentor. Make sure that they have heard you present. Also, make sure that they have a positive attitude rather than being too critical. Ask them to rate you honestly using the assessment statements listed above. Make a note of their ratings.

Are their ratings similar to yours? Where have they rated you higher or lower than you have? Without taking offence or getting defensive, discuss with them why they rated you as they did.

This is a valuable check as to how others perceive us. It is said that perception is reality. You may think you are communicating just fine, but others may have a different opinion. On the other hand, you may think you are a nervous speaker, whereas your audience actually feels that you come across as a confident speaker.

Take note of these perceptions and see whether you need to focus on some areas for development more than others.

Confidence is a Magical Ingredient

Having confidence can change a person's outlook. Confidence can change perception. Confidence can change lives. When you have confidence, suddenly the world seems a different place – as happened with twelve-year-old John.

A DAVID BECKHAM IN THE MAKING?

John was part of a Sydney school's under-thirteen soccer team.

One of my family members played on the same team as John and so I went along to support them each week. The team included three boys who were, let's say, athletically challenged. John in particular could not wait to *get off* the field. Every few minutes he would ask the coach 'How long to go?' or 'Can I get substituted?' *or* 'I'm not feeling good. Can I come off?'

One could plainly see that John did not enjoy playing soccer. The team was not enjoying the games either, as they were being hammered *6-0, 10-0, 20-0.*

As John came off the field one day after another demoralising defeat, I overheard him say, 'I hate soccer. I'm crap at it.'

And then one morning, one magical morning, everything changed. I can't really say what caused it. Perhaps all the boys had a double serving of Weetbix. But they had come to play. It started off with a great save from the goalkeeper. Then I noticed all the boys encouraging each other. In particular they were encouraging the athletically challenged boys. There seemed to be a renewed spirit among the whole team.

'Great kick, Tom.'

'Good defence Rob, good defence'

'Great pass John. Good one mate.'

And then the parents joined in the encouragement. It was heart-warming stuff. John in particular started off with small wins. Each time he kicked the ball, or blocked a defender, or did a throw-in from the sidelines, he received a cheer from the small crowd.

At half-time the score was 1-0 to the opposition. You could see the relief on the boys' faces. Today, maybe, just maybe they would not be beaten by a cricket score. The coach was clearly pleased and encouraged the boys to attack more and win the game.

I could see John becoming more confident. He was certainly not asking the coach when he could come off. Instead of passively waiting for the ball to come to him, he actively went in search of the ball. When an attacker went past him, he pursued the attacker and valiantly tried to get the ball off him. And often John succeeded in doing this.

With five minutes to the end of the game, the score was still 1-0 to the opposition. It was then that John got the ball around mid-field and gave the striker a wonderful pass that dissected two opposition players. The striker seized the opportunity, dribbled the ball up to the penalty area and kicked with all his might past the goalkeeper and into the back of the net.

Wow! What a celebration. The boys were giving high-fives to the striker and John. The parents went a little wild. After all it was the first goal of the season! John was beaming from ear to ear. Nothing was going to take that smile off him.

The game ended at 1-1. But what a great feeling as the boys congratulated each other and the coach had some wonderful accolades to offer.

I went up to John while he was getting ready to go home with his mother. I said 'Great game, John. You played fantastic soccer. Well done.'

He replied with a smile 'Yeah, I really enjoyed the game. That's the first time I've enjoyed it. I don't know why.'

I smiled and thought to myself, *I know why*. John had accidentally discovered the magical ingredient that David Beckham oozes. *Confidence!*

Jamaican leader Marcus Garvey put it succinctly: 'With

confidence you have won before you have started.'

In the next chapter we explore the arch-enemy of confidence: Fear.

Summary

1. Recognise the difference between confidence and arrogance: arrogant people are self-centred and often want to be the only winner; confident people are focused on others and want everyone to win.

2. Great speakers are confident, calm, always in control, and know that their message has value to others.

3. When self-assessing your speaking capabilities, get a second opinion from a trusted source and compare your ratings. Remember, others' perception of you is reality.

4. Confidence is magical and can change your outlook on life! Become confident, read on!

CHAPTER 2

Why Fear is a Speaker's Nightmare

'There is no illusion greater than fear.'

LAO TZU

The arch-enemy of confidence is fear. It is said that we are born with only two fears: the fear of loud noises and the fear of falling down. I had first-hand experience of the loud noises theory a few years ago with my little niece. She was at the crawling stage. One day she was crawling down the corridor oblivious to the world, when I crept up behind her and startled her with a loud 'Boo'. I thought she was going to giggle. But the laugh was on *me* when she paused for a couple of seconds before bursting into a wailing scream. I don't think she's ever forgiven me for that.

All other fears are manifested through our life experiences. The main fears for most people are the fear of failure and the fear of rejection. As a young man, I knew these fears well. I grew up in a very conservative Catholic environment. My parents were very protective of their children.

> *'Don't play with that knife. It will cut you and you will bleed to death.'*

> *'Be careful who you go out with.'*

> *'Don't stay out too late. It's too dangerous.'*

While this advice was intended to shield us, it also had a negative effect on me. I was too afraid to try new things. I was petrified of taking a risk. I played it safe most of the time. I lived the Uninspired Speaker's life. *Safe*, but very *boring*.

Pass or Fail

Most of our life is judged by a pass or fail. As students we are rated by the education system. We pass or we fail.

At work we are judged through our annual performance appraisals. Pass or fail.

At sport we are judged through our wins or losses.

No prizes for coming second.

Win at all costs.

Winners are grinners. Losers whinge about the referee.

Pass or fail.

No wonder so many people suffer from the fear of failure. Each time they are judged, the fear of failure rears its ugly head.

ONE TOUGH MANAGER

I have personally experienced the fear of failure many times. Some of those experiences smashed my esteem. A few years ago as an employee in the corporate world, I had the performance appraisal from hell. A new manager had assumed control of the team that I was part of. She was a tough, no-nonsense person, great at what she did with exceedingly high expectations of all her staff.

At my performance appraisal, she made it very clear that she was unhappy with my performance and that it was sub-standard. I was shocked and upset because this was the first I had been made aware of her view. But I was more upset because my pride was dented. I wanted to do a good job. Few people go out of their way to do a bad job.

This appraisal had a devastating effect on my morale. My self-esteem had taken a bullet. I felt lost and wallowed in self-pity. Instead of being more proactive I played safer, trying to fly under the radar. This approach was not delivering the right results and my esteem took another nose-dive at the next half-yearly appraisal.

Fortunately for me, the manager was also a very intelligent woman. She saw how the low self-esteem continued to impact my work performance and she devised a course of action. We agreed on the action plan and she proceeded to provide her full support.

I started to get results, small wins at first. These wins made me feel good and increased my esteem. Soon I was taking on more challenging work and succeeding at it. Another boost to my self-esteem! I ended that year with a great performance appraisal and feeling really good about myself. I felt that I had licked the fear of failure and it was all due to a manager who was tough but fair.

The Fear of Failure and You

How about you? Have you encountered the fear of failure? Has it had an impact on your self-esteem?

Often the people we look up to, the role models in our life, can be the instigators of the fear of failure. Perhaps your parents wanted you to be a doctor or a lawyer but you chose another path. Or like me, your manager had different expectations about your performance than you did. These negative experiences can instill the fear of failure.

FEAR OF FAILURE AND GUILT

The fear of failure may be magnified when role models have expectations of us that are different from our own. Then we feel guilty. I joke with my Catholic friends about Catholic guilt. Those of you who are Catholic may identify with these guilt-inducers:

Not attending church on Sundays.

Eating meat on Friday during Lent.

Not contributing to the collection plate.

Enough about Catholics. And I promise to go to confession … soon!

Feelings of guilt can impact on our self-esteem. At this point, simply be aware of people attempting to make you feel guilty. Strategies for building confidence will help you overcome this.

FEAR OF REJECTION

The fear of rejection is right up there with the fear of failure. In fact the two are grim brothers in arms. The fear of rejection is due to human beings wanting to belong and be accepted. Most of us want to belong: to a family, to a community, to work groups. When we have a sense of belonging, we feel validated. We also want to feel validated by the role models and mentors in our lives. If these role models do not affirm us, we may encounter feelings of rejection. These role models (such as parents, teachers and managers) can play a big part in how we feel and what we do as a result of what they say.

LUCY'S PREDICAMENT

A few years ago I was part of a voluntary group of facilitators running a half-day public speaking workshop for Rotarian Youth. There were about a hundred participants and during one segment each facilitator was required to manage a group of fifteen young people.

My role as facilitator was to provide each participant in my group with an impromptu topic to speak on and then lead a discussion on how they performed. One young woman, Lucy, appeared really nervous but answered the topic quite well. The rest of the group and I gave Lucy some great encouragement.

I then asked for a volunteer to do a speech for five minutes in front of the entire Rotarian group of 100. Lucy put up her hand and said that she would do it. We spent some time supporting her and developing the message. Then it was show time.

Lucy got up and gave a very credible performance on her passion: skiing. She received a standing ovation from the group. She bounded up to me afterwards and asked for feedback on her performance. I told her what I considered she did well and provided her with a couple of points for improvement.

It was then that she said to me 'Mark, I'm so glad I attended this workshop. It has restored my confidence.'

I said 'Restored your confidence? What do you mean?'

Lucy responded 'When I was in Year 10, I gave a speech during a speech contest. My teacher said that it was a terrible speech and that I should focus my efforts elsewhere. Since then, I have never given another speech because I thought I was pathetic at it. Today, I was so nervous about doing the impromptu topic but when I received wonderful encouragement from everyone, I thought maybe I'm not so bad. Then I surprised myself by volunteering to do the main speech. And now that I've done it I feel really good. In fact, I feel great. In such a short time, I feel my confidence restored.'

Wow! Can you *imagine?* What a great result to what could have been a totally different experience for Lucy.

It is sad that a teacher could be so negative, not understanding the devastating impact of such a comment. For five years Lucy believed that her teacher, a role model, knew more than she did about her presenting abilities. Lucy felt she could never speak well, so she shied away from it. If Lucy had not attended that workshop and had her self-esteem restored, how many great messages from Lucy would people have missed out on in the future?

Have you ever experienced what Lucy did? Has someone ever rubbished the way you presented or not provided encouragement?

If you suffer from low self-esteem it is easy to accept what others say, and it can seem as if everyone has an opinion. But sometimes that opinion is from people who do not have experience, or are not well informed or well considered.

Don't let anyone tell you that you cannot. Know that you can do anything that you aspire to do. Consider these actions:

- Just trust yourself;

- Learn as much as you can;

- Get professional help from a life coach or training from an expert in your field of endeavour;

- Take positive action, just as Lucy did.

Fight or Flight

The fight-or-flight response was first described by Walter Cannon, a US physiologist in 1929. His theory states that animals react to threats with a general discharge of the sympathetic nervous system priming the animal for fighting or fleeing.

In prehistoric times when the fight-or-flight response evolved, fight was manifested in aggressive, combative behaviour and flight was manifested by fleeing potentially threatening situations, such as being confronted by a predator. In current times, these responses still exist, but they exhibit a wider range of behaviours. For example, the fight response may be manifested in angry, argumentative behaviour, and the flight response may be manifested through social withdrawal, substance abuse, and even locking oneself in a room.

The fight-or-flight response is particularly prevalent when people are required to speak to an audience.

A DOCTOR'S CALL

A few years ago, I received a call for help from a GP who had a patient encountering major distress because of his reaction to doing presentations. The patient, David, was a senior executive in the finance industry. Each time David was asked to do a presentation he would become anxious weeks in advance of speech day. As the day approached, the impact on him became worse. He would get headaches, feel nauseous and often retch. Most times he would call in sick on presentation day, because he really did feel sick. He would then go to his GP to obtain a medical certificate. His GP tried a few options but none seemed to successfully cure David. This is when the GP suggested that David needed help with his public speaking and approached me.

When I met David, I discovered one of the worst cases of public speaking nerves I'd ever seen. It was a classic flight response.

David was in his mid-thirties and had a young family. As a senior manager he was expected to do numerous speaking engagements. He was a talented and ambitious individual and was promoted due to his technical abilities. But the higher up the corporate ladder he climbed, the more he was expected to speak to groups.

As a young man, David had some bad experiences with public speaking both at school and as an apprentice. The positive influences in David's life were few and far between. His self-esteem was low. He'd worked very hard to get to where he was, but he still had the scars of his youth and shied away from public speaking opportunities because of his *fear of failure* and *fear of rejection*.

At our first meeting, David was desperate for help. I can still see the forlorn look in his eyes as he almost pleaded 'Can you help me?'

Of course I said yes.

David was looking for a trusted advisor and coach. We worked on many of the confidence techniques that I share in the next chapter. David began to act on all of the strategies I suggested. He was the perfect student: attentive, eager to learn, action oriented.

When he was ready, David started to do more presentations. Little steps at first. A presentation to his *spouse*. A presentation to his *family*. A presentation to his *small team*.

This gave him the confidence to move to bigger challenges. After a few months, David had proudly progressed to speaking before his company board. This board consisted of some household names in the Australian business world.

It took a while but David had finally managed to deal with his demons. He had *conquered* his Goliath.

Some of the world's most famous people have admitted to anxiety attacks and stage fright. These include actor Johnny Depp, singer Cher and even scientist Sir Isaac Newton. Mark Twain said it best: *'There are two types of speakers: those that are nervous and those that are liars.'*

Everyone, even experienced speakers, has some anxiety when speaking in front of a group of people. This is perfectly normal. The best way to deal with this anxiety is first to acknowledge that this fear is normal and you are not alone. Once you have acknowledged the fear then you can move on to increasing your confidence.

CHAPTER 3

How to Build Confidence

> '*When you have confidence, you can have a lot of fun. And when you have fun, you can do amazing things.*'
>
> JOE NAMATH,
> AMERICAN FOOTBALL QUARTERBACK

Let's then have ourselves some fun!

In the next few chapters we will explore strategies to increase your confidence so that you too can discover its magic and use it to change your perceptions and perhaps even change your life.

Review each strategy and apply it to building your esteem and confidence. These strategies have worked for millions around the world, trust that they will work for you. Follow the instructions positively and often. Give them a chance to work. The results will have a positive impact on you and will greatly increase your confidence levels.

Build Confidence with Affirmations

Psychologists say that we *speak* at the rate of 150 words per minute, but we *self-talk* at the rate of 600 words a minute. Self-talk is where you 'talk' in your mind. You make *judgments* in your mind. You *review* and *assess* in your mind. Basically, self-talk is an internal dialogue that can have a *positive* or *negative* influence upon you.

THE DANGER OF SELF-TALK

The danger of self-talk is that we may use it as a negative influencing tool. Often we tend to be self-critical. We beat ourselves up and imagine results before they happen.

In a presenting context we may *sabotage* ourselves.

'What if the audience doesn't like me?'

'What if I look stupid in front of my peers?'

'I'll stuff up if I forget my lines.'

At 600 words a minute, we are *crucifying* ourselves. That is a lot of self-torture throughout our lives. The longer we hammer ourselves, the harder it gets to lift out of our negative environment to a more positive setting. A positive setting is where we feel comfortable with who we are, forgive our shortcomings, focus on constructive outcomes and begin to live an optimistic life.

PESSIMISM AND REALISM VERSUS OPTIMISM

I often laugh internally (along with good old self-talk) when I hear someone say 'I am not a pessimist. I'm a realist.' To me, a realist leans quite hard against its close cousin, the pessimist. I have yet to hear a self-proclaimed realist say 'The world is a great place.' You're more likely to hear 'Reality is that the world is full of challenges. But I am not a pessimist.'

DECISION TIME: WHERE DO YOU STAND?

So, the first thing to decide is where you stand. Do you consider yourself a pessimist, a realist or an optimist? If you lean towards being a pessimist or a realist, then I encourage you to re-think your stance.

Pessimists and realists often focus on the *problems* and *challenges* facing them. Optimists focus on *opportunities*.

A woman I worked with once complained to me 'My husband and I hate his parents attitude. The in-laws are so happy all the time. They are optimists. They need to get a reality check.' Criticised for being happy and optimistic! Rather, the in-laws should be unhappy and pessimistic (or realistic) so that this woman and her husband would feel more comfortable.

Be careful of your surroundings. Who do you associate with? Are your associates optimists? Or are they pessimistic in their outlook on life?

Pessimists will tend to bring you down to their level. They are more comfortable when people around them are not succeeding as it makes them feel normal. If you succeed, they will start to get uncomfortable that you are winning and they are not. They may also wallow in a 'woe is me' attitude. This is a dangerous place for you to be as their gravity will swiftly yank you down into their world. Try to extricate yourself from pessimists as they can be draining and hard work.

Seek out friends or work colleagues who display optimistic behaviours. If they are genuinely optimistic, they will *welcome* you. They will be *good role models* for you.

They will *inspire* you.

WHAT TO DO IF FAMILY MEMBERS ARE PESSIMISTS?

I am often asked this question. We can choose our friends and work colleagues to an extent but we can't choose our family.

If you do have a pessimist in the family, firstly be aware of this tendency to bring you down and make a decision not to be affected by what they say. Do not preach to them the virtues of being an optimist. Instead, work on your own positive attitude. Gain small wins that will help your confidence levels. When you have sufficient confidence, try to subtly help the pessimistic family member. If this does not work, then just continue to be unaffected by what they say.

WHAT ARE AFFIRMATIONS?

Affirmations are simply positive statements. You can affirm that you are a *good person*. Affirm that you are a *positive individual*. Affirm that you are a *valuable employee*.

Most professional athletes use affirmations. They use positive statements to constantly reinforce how capable they are. These athletes know that the more they use affirmations, the less chance there is of negative self-talk. They are essentially replacing the negative self-talk with positive affirmations.

Imagine the results. Rather than self-talking yourself *down*, you are self-talking yourself *up!* Affirmations can change your outlook on life and boost confidence. *Don't spank yourself, high-five yourself!*

HOW I AFFIRMED MYSELF TO SUCCESS

In the introduction to this book, I talked about how I moved from the *Uninspired Speakers* path, back up to the fork in the road. It was then that I came across the power of affirmations. I learnt about affirmations from a series of tapes by Brian Tracy called *The Psychology of Achievement*. This was one of my first introductions to self-development and it had an enormous impact on my attitude and outlook on life.

To overcome my fear of public speaking, I developed this simple affirmation.

'I am a confident speaker.'

Each business day I used to drive ten minutes to the local train station. I used these ten minutes morning and afternoon to religiously affirm myself. In the quietness of my car, with no distractions, I affirmed aloud.

'I am a confident speaker. I am a confident speaker. I am a confident speaker.'

Prior to doing any speech, I found a quiet place and affirmed aloud:

'I am a confident speaker. I am a confident speaker. I am a confident speaker.'

Before long, these affirmations were like a recording in my head. Just like a good song that you keep humming to yourself long after the song is over. That's how this affirmation played in my mind.

My confidence increased dramatically. I started to speak to large groups of people. I entered public speaking contests. I was invited as a guest speaker to various functions. The more I *affirmed*, the more confident I became. The more *confident* I became, the more I presented. The more I *presented*, the more *doors opened*.

I was well on my way to becoming a *confident* and *effective* speaker.

RULES FOR AFFIRMATIONS

Here are three simple rules for affirmations.

RULE ONE:
Write Down Your Affirmation and Read It Out Loud

When you first say an affirmation, I strongly suggest that you write it out on a small card and then read it out aloud.

The reason for doing this is that you are using the two main learning senses: sight and sound. You are seeing the words on the card and hearing yourself affirm.

Once you feel comfortable with your affirmation, there is no real need to use the card to see the words, because the affirmation will be imprinted in your mind. You can then just say the affirmation aloud (or in your mind if you are around people). Use the power of positive self-talk to constantly affirm yourself.

RULE TWO:
Always Affirm in the Present Tense

By affirming in the present tense, you are tricking your subconscious mind into believing what you are saying is true.

If you use the past tense, saying 'I was a confident speaker', or future tense, 'I will be a confident speaker', then your subconscious mind will not believe it is true right now. So, always use present tense: '*I am* a confident speaker'.

If you say it often enough, then your subconscious mind will believe it and it becomes a self-fulfilling prophecy.

RULE THREE:
Affirm with Great Emotion
This is probably the most crucial element of saying affirmations. Imagine saying in an emotionless and dreary voice 'I am an inspiration to others.'

Do you think your subconscious mind would believe you? No!

However saying the same affirmation with great emotion, perhaps placing emphasis on the key words, in this case 'am' and 'inspiration', will make the affirmation much more believable. So use immense emotion when you are affirming.

'I am an inspiration to others.'

'I am an inspiration to others.'

'I am an inspiration to others.'

What are you?

Correct. An inspiration to others!

HOW DAVID USED AFFIRMATIONS
In the previous chapter I wrote about David, a senior executive who overcame his public-speaking fears. One of the techniques David used very effectively was saying affirmations.

David had a long drive from Sydney's northern suburbs to

the city each day. He used this valuable time to affirm and this is what he said each day:

'I am a confident and capable person in all that I do.'

He told me that this really pumped him up each day. Saying the affirmation was an energy booster for his mind and body especially first thing in the morning.

Affirmations work. They worked for David and have worked for millions of others. If you have not used affirmations before, then I would fully encourage you to start now. Let the power of self-talk work for you and not against you.

STARTING YOUR AFFIRMATION

Now that you know the rules of affirmations, commit to a suitable affirmation for you.

Firstly, decide the outcome that you want. Do you want to be a valuable employee? Or do you aspire to be a great entrepreneur? How about a confident speaker?

Next, write down all the possible affirmations that you think will help you achieve that outcome. Choose one and make sure that it is stated in the present tense.

Then start to practise your affirmation. The more it rhymes, the better. Use it like a mantra. It should be easy to say without any tongue twisters. Change it if you think of something that makes you feel more comfortable.

Start using it every day. Find a good time slot so that you can do it as a habit. Perhaps first thing in the morning when you wake up or when are in the car on your journey to work. Perhaps in a quiet place at lunchtime. Or in the evening after dinner and away from family members.

Try not to miss an opportunity to say your affirmations.

Remember, all those positive words will make a positive impact on your life.

EXAMPLES OF AFFIRMATIONS

Here are some examples of affirmations from a great friend and outstanding speaker, Ken Bernard.

'My thoughts are pure and positive.'

'My dreams come true.'

'I radiate self-esteem and wellbeing.'

'Good things come to me easily.'

'I live an abundant life.'

'Everything I do brings growth.'

Summary

1. Decide to be an optimist and surround yourself with optimists.

2. Affirmations are a great way to see the good in you and help you move you towards your goal.

3. Commit to identifying affirmations that are suitable for you. Base your affirmations on the outcome you want.

4. Write down all the possible affirmations that meet your end outcome. Narrow your choice to a single affirmation and make sure that it is stated in the present tense.

5. Start to practice your affirmation. If it rhymes, all the better. Use it like a mantra.

6. Affirm every day. Find a suitable time slot and make it a habit.

Build Confidence with Visualisation

'Part of my preparation is I go and ask the kit man what colour we're wearing – if it's red top, white shorts, white socks or black socks. Then I lie in bed the night before the game and visualise myself scoring goals or doing well.'

Wayne Rooney (England's star goal scorer)

The Sydney Olympic Games in 2000 will be forever etched in my memory as one of the greatest sporting events I have witnessed. I was lucky enough to be in the stadium to see some great moments including Cathy Freeman's incredible win in the Women's 400m final, and US athlete Maurice Greene win the Men's 100m final. What struck me was Greene's preparation just prior to the event. The big screens in the stadium showed a close-up of Greene preparing for the race of his life. In seemed clear to me that he was visualising his run and winning the gold medal. His eyes were so focused, it looked like he was hypnotised. After a few minutes of visualisation, he appeared more relaxed. He was ready, and how! Greene brilliantly won the gold medal that night and I think visualisation helped play some part in his victory.

How about you? Do you visualise success? Like affirmations, visualisation is just another tool to increase confidence. Visualisation helps you to prepare for the real experience.

AFFIRMATIONS VERSUS VISUALISATION

The key difference between affirmations and visualisation is when to use these tools.

The value of affirmations is that they can and should be used every day to affirm your success.

Visualisation is best used for a specific event; it could be a specific sports event, or a particular job interview or even a speech before an audience.

HOW VISUALISATION HELPED IMPROVE MY SPEAKING

Visualisation has been a vital tool to help me 'preview' a successful experience. Each time I have to present to an audience I use visualisation techniques to support my preparation.

In my mind's eye I see exactly what I'm going to wear during the presentation.

I see myself step up to the platform and confidently stride to the centre. I visualise myself warmly shaking hands with the MC. I see myself presenting with great confidence to the audience. The audience is connecting with my message with frequent nods, laughs and raised hands for questions.

Then I visualise the end. The audience greatly appreciates my message with enthusiastic ovation. I feel the pride of giving a great presentation and satisfaction that is has provided outstanding value to my audience.

Visualisation techniques have been immensely successful for me and I am sure that they will increase your confidence levels too.

RULES FOR VISUALISATION

Here are three simple rules for visualisation.

RULE ONE: **Visualise the Event in Detail**

When you visualise add as much detail as you can. Imagine you are watching a movie with yourself in the starring role! Visualise in colour. Visualise the exact clothes that you will wear. Visualise the movements that you will make, the eye contact, the body language. Visualise the people you are meeting or presenting to. See their faces, create their reactions.

RULE TWO: **Visualise a Positive Experience**

When you visualise, always see yourself in a positive light. Picture a positive experience and a great outcome. See the outcome you want; perhaps it's winning a race, or receiving an award or even getting a standing ovation for a great presentation. In this scenario, see your listeners applauding vigorously, smiling back at you and really appreciating your message to them. See yourself winning!

RULE THREE: **Feel the Emotion of Winning**

See yourself winning and feel the *emotion* of winning. Create the pride you will feel when you win. *Feel* the joy of winning. *Feel* your blood rushing, pumping through your veins, *feel* your chest expanding with great pride, *feel* the wonderful positive energy you have as a result of your tremendous win!

Feeling the emotion of winning is a vital component of visualisation – use this effective technique to build confidence towards your speaking success.

WHAT IF I DON'T WIN?

There will be times when no matter how much you visualise success, it will not eventuate. Not everyone can win a race even though all competitors are visualising success. Visualisation is preparing you to do your best. Visualisation increases the odds, even if you may not achieve the success you desire on that particular occasion.

Stick with visualisation, even if it's just used to boost confidence. The more you use this technique, the more confident you will become. The ultimate outcome you want at this stage is increased confidence – success will follow.

Summary

To visualise success, follow these rules:

1. Visualise in detail. Visualise in colour, see all the movements, simulate what you will do in preparation for the real event.

2. Visualise winning. Visualise the outcome you desire. See yourself winning.

3. Feel that winning emotion. Feel the joy and pride you have when you win!

4. Don't give up on visualisation. Use it as a confidence-building tool and know that success will come!

Six Confidence-Building Strategies

Here are six more simple but highly effective strategies to build confidence.

START A SUCCESS FOLDER

A great way to increase your confidence is to start a Success Folder. This folder can be used to capture all your successes. It could be successes at work, with your hobby or achievements with your family and friends.

For healthy self-esteem, it is important that you start to recognise all the wins you have made along life's journey. Small wins will make you feel good and inspire you to greater challenges. If you don't feel you had a win in a certain situation, then that's OK too. In that case, you can learn from the experience, and use the learning to build confidence for your next challenge. The wins will come. And when they do come, add them to your success folder.

Recently I completed a six-month consulting contract. As I tidied up loose ends, I came across numerous online folders that contained documents I produced as part of the consultancy. I was amazed how many there were and the positive impact of the work. When you are working every day, you may lose sight of all the good work you have achieved. You forget about the small wins. All of those small wins mean something. They all add up to enhancing your self-esteem and boosting your confidence.

So, start your Success Folder right away. Add to it as soon as you accomplish something of value, however small. At the end of each month, take stock and review your achievements. Feel good about the value you have created in your life. Keep doing it and see your confidence grow.

LAUGH BIG

How often do you smile? How many times a day do you laugh out loud?

Laughter is universal. There are thousands of languages, hundreds of thousands of dialects, but everybody laughs in pretty much the same way.

The more you laugh, the more comfortable you feel within yourself. The more comfortable you feel within yourself, the more confident you become.

Scientific research demonstrates that laughter offers the following benefits:

- Lowering blood pressure;

- Strengthening cardiovascular functions;

- Reducing stress hormones;

- Improving circulation;

- Increasing muscle flexion;

- Oxygenating the body by boosting the respiratory system;

- Triggering the release of endorphins, the body's natural painkillers;

- Producing a general sense of wellbeing.

If you are serious by nature, then try to change your demeanour and see if you can increase opportunities to laugh. People often reflect the person they are interacting with, so, if you put on a grumpy or frowning face, people may reflect that back at you.

Mr. Serious

A friend once confided in me that he was annoyed at people frowning at him: people on the train, people at the supermarket counter, people at work meetings. I asked him if he normally smiled at these people. He reflected and said 'No, I'm normally serious looking, perhaps even frowning.' I didn't need to say another word. He had an *epiphany!*

If you welcome people with a nice big smile, then they will most often reflect a nice big smile right back at you. This makes everyone feel good. So, cultivate a smiling habit.

Self-Deprecating Humour

Wikipedia defines self-deprecating humour as humour which relies on the observation of something negative about the person delivering it. Many comedians use self-deprecating humour to avoid seeming arrogant or pompous, and to help the audience identify with them.

If it works for comedians, then why not make it work for you?

Too often we are eager to beat ourselves up or be critical of others. Try self-deprecating humour at these times. Don't take yourself too seriously. Commit to having fun. Have fun with others. Have fun with yourself. Become a fun junky!

Laughing with Others

A few years ago, I experienced a discomforting situation with two of my work colleagues. They were firm friends with each other and it seemed that they were out to make snide comments about me at every opportunity. A colleague suggested that I didn't take their remarks personally and, instead, tried to connect with them. So, I started to be pleasant and then joke with them. It didn't take long for them to reciprocate. We changed our relationship through laughter and eventually became good work friends.

It is said that the measure of a good relationship is how much you are laughing with the person. Are you laughing a lot with your partner? Are you laughing with your work colleagues? Are you laughing with your friends? Improve your relationships. *Start laughing big!*

USE NAMES

One of my favourite self-development books is *How to Win Friends and Influence People* by Dale Carnegie. In this classic, Mr. Carnegie strongly recommends using people's names when conversing.

This single recommendation has added significant depth to how I connect with others. People love to hear their own name. I'm sure you do too. But how often do you hear it when people are conversing with you?

1001 Interviews

I have spent many years in the corporate world and have participated in numerous interviews both as an interviewer and interviewee. I always use the person's name when I am communicating with them. In conversation I often listen out for people to mention my name.

How many do it? Less than five percent! I am astounded that such a simple thing is overlooked by so many. It is also interesting to note that most of the people who do use other peoples' names when conversing are also confident people. They are confident in their own abilities and comfortable addressing others during conversation.

Why say a person's name? When you use a person's name,

you are firstly obtaining their attention. You are also showing respect because you remember their name. Saying their name frequently indicates that you like them enough to use it and therefore increases your chances of being liked back.

If people like you, then you feel good about yourself. This increases your confidence.

So, say other people's names as often as you can in conversations. Practice first with your own family. Then extend this to all your conversations no matter with whom.

MAKE A GOOD FIRST IMPRESSION

You've heard the saying '*first impressions count*'. This is so true, particularly as you start to build confidence. If you make a good first impression, people are more likely to receive you positively. They are more likely to treat you with respect and engage in conversation with you. One of the first impressions people make of you is based on how you look.

For my fortieth birthday I gave myself a present: an ear piercing to accommodate a diamond stud. Perhaps it was a mid-life crisis type of present, but I can assure you it was a lot cheaper than buying a Harley Davidson.

I was working for a large corporation at the time, and wearing an earring there was probably frowned upon, particularly by the more conservative senior managers. Perhaps I was self-conscious but I remember the looks I would receive when meeting business people for the first time. I felt I was being judged immediately because of the earring.

After a few months I decided that, working in the banking industry, the earring was doing me no favours, so I removed it during business hours. Why disadvantage myself? First impressions, rightly or wrongly, do count. People make judgments often and they make them instantly. So keep this in mind and stack the odds in your favour.

The Importance of Eye Contact

Making eye contact is a challenge for some people. They may feel that eye contact is off-putting, or the same as glaring, and even perceive it as a sign of aggression. If you feel like this, then make eye contact with care. What does that mean? It means keep direct eye contact but blink normally, smile appropriately, and, of course, behave in a non-aggressive manner.

Making eye contact is a sign of how confident a person is. If you do not make eye contact, it may be perceived that you are lying or trying to hide something.

A few years ago, a colleague and I were interviewing a candidate for a job. Each of us took turns to ask him questions. I noticed something very interesting. All of his responses were made to my colleague regardless of whether she was asking the questions or I was asking them.

After the interview, I made an observation to my colleague that the candidate avoided eye contact with me throughout the interview. She countered with 'I thought he made great eye contact when answering the questions.' Of course, she would have thought that.

So, in this situation, remember to make eye contact with all of the people on the interview panel to ensure that you are connecting with all the decision makers.

Cultural Differences

People from certain backgrounds may have trouble maintaining eye contact when speaking. I was raised in such a culture and was taught as a child not to make eye contact as a sign of respect for elders or people in authority. If this applies to you too, then keep in mind the phrase 'When in Rome, do as the Romans do.' This means that if you are living and working in a Western country, don't put yourself at a disadvantage by not maintaining eye contact.

Handshakes

Have you ever shaken someone's hand and felt them almost crush your palm? Or worse, shaken a hand that felt like you were shaking a wet, limp fish?

Handshakes are universally used in meetings, greetings, and in offering congratulations. Handshakes are a sign of trust and help build good relationships.

A firm handshake says a lot about you. Always maintain a positive handshake that complements a nice warm smile, and bear in mind the following tips:

- Before the handshake, make sure you palms are not sweaty. Use a paper towel to remove any moisture.

- If your hands are cold, then try to warm them by rubbing them together. If they are still cold at the time you shake hands, offer an apology to the recipient. You can also make a joke if it's appropriate, such as 'cold hands, warm heart'.

- Shake hands with men and women the same way.

- Remember, the best handshakes are firm, brief and accompanied by a smile.

How to Do a Good Handshake

- As you approach the recipient, extend your right arm when you are about a metre away. Your arm should be in an L-shape and slightly in front of you with your thumb pointing up.

- Lock hands, thumb joint to thumb joint.

- Firmly clasp the other person's hand. Remember no bone crushing or show of machismo.

- Shake their hand straight up and down two or three times and then release.

WALK WITH PURPOSE

Have you noticed how successful people walk a little faster or with a greater sense of purpose than most of the general population? Working in the Sydney CBD for many years, I have witnessed many CEOs and politicians, such as former Australian prime ministers John Howard and Tony Abbott, walk, and they always appear to stride with purpose.

Why is walking with purpose a confidence builder?

Walking with purpose *signals* that you are a busy person. Time is of the essence. You are going somewhere and need to get there fast. If you walk with purpose, people may perceive you as busy and important. And perception is everything.

Another reason why walking faster is beneficial is that it gets the blood circulating more. It energises you. And if it energises you, then that may contribute to making you feel good about yourself and increase your self-esteem.

From today, start to observe how leaders walk. I guarantee

you that they won't be dawdling. They will be walking in earnest, with purpose.

Try it yourself. This really is a great way to increase your confidence. Make it a habit to walk that little bit faster. Feel the difference to your confidence.

USE EVERY OPPORTUNITY TO SPEAK

Reading books is fine. Listening to theory is also great. But nothing beats actually taking action, putting theories into practice. W. Clement Stone put it perfectly: *'Thinking will not overcome fear but action will.'* Taking *action* will help overcome fear and instill confidence. Speak at every opportunity, learn and keep improving.

How a Basketball Star Spoke at Every Opportunity

Many years ago I met Damian Keogh at a business conference where he presented the keynote address. Mr. Keogh is an ex-Sydney Kings basketball star and wore the Australian green and gold colours with pride on more than 200 occasions. When I met him, Mr. Keogh had retired from pro basketball and was doing the professional speaking circuit as a motivational speaker.

During his address, he often had his listeners in stitches of laughter and they really connected with his message on teamwork. After his presentation, I approached Mr. Keogh and asked him how he became such a wonderful speaker. He very humbly replied that he learnt his craft by presenting his message hundreds of times a year. This meant he was constantly able to refine his message and his presentation style.

It didn't surprise me that Mr. Keogh presented so often. He

followed the same format of constant practice as he did during his pro basketball days. Hour *after* hour of practice. Day *after* day. That's why Damian Keogh represented Australia so many times. That's why he was in such great demand as a professional speaker.

One of the ways Damian Keogh increased his confidence was by speaking as many times as he could. I encourage you to look for the same opportunities to present.

But Where to Present?

Here are some speaking opportunities for you to consider:

- Join a public speaking organisation like Toastmasters International and practise your speeches there.

- Rotary and Lions Clubs are other organisations that offer opportunities to speak.

- If you attend a church, you can volunteer to do the readings.

- If your children go to school, volunteer to speak to their class. My children were so proud when I did this.

- If your child plays sport, belongs to scouts or guides, or has another relevant hobby, volunteer to present at one of their sessions.

- At any family or work function, volunteer to do one of the informal speeches. My bet is that you will get snapped up immediately as there are often few takers for this role.

- And finally, here's a real easy one. Invite your family

or friends over for a pizza night, and present to them. They'll listen to anything as long as they get free pizza!

There are hundreds of opportunities available (or that you can manufacture) to present. Use as many as possible. It will be like magic to feel your confidence soar as you journey towards success.

Summary

To build confidence:

1. Start a Success Folder. Include small wins, big wins, all wins. Feel pride in all of your accomplishments.

2. Laugh. Release the tension, increase endorphins and bring joy to yourself and others. Make laughter a daily habit.

3. Use people's names. Connect with people simply by addressing them in the course of conversation. They'll like you more for it.

4. Make a good first impression. Dress to impress, make eye contact and have a warm, welcoming handshake.

5. Walk with purpose. Successful people do. This will raise your energy levels and make you feel important too.

6. Present often. Find opportunities to speak to small groups and this will build your confidence.

CHAPTER 4

Learn the Secrets of Confident Speakers

'Confidence comes from hours and days and weeks and years of constant work and dedication.'

ROGER STAUBACH

In this chapter we will explore further techniques to build confidence. These techniques are frequently employed by professional and experienced speakers.

Never Wing It

One way to make sure you deliver with confidence is to practise your speech. Even great speakers don't leave anything to chance. Here's a lesson from one of them.

A few years ago I hosted a dinner for ten Westpac Banking

Group graduates who had successfully completed a public speaking program. At the time, the Westpac CEO was US-born Bob Joss. Mr. Joss was well known for his focus on self-development and encouraging the bank's employees to do the same. I invited Mr. Joss to present the graduates with their certificates of completion for the public speaking program. The graduates were delighted when he accepted.

Mr. Joss gave up his lunchtime to join us at a Chinese restaurant in the city. After the certificates were presented, Mr. Joss was happy to answer questions from the graduates. One of them asked him if he ever winged a speech.

Mr. Joss replied, 'I have never winged a speech nor dare I wing one in future. As a presenter and a leader, if you wing a speech, the audience will see right through you. By winging a presentation, you are also disrespecting the audience because you are essentially saying that you could not be bothered taking the time to prepare to present to them. My advice to you is never, ever wing it.'

Well, there you have it. If a CEO with the experience of Mr. Joss never wings a speech, then we can certainly learn from his sage words. Never, ever wing it!

No Substitute for Practice

Real estate's motto is 'location, location, location.' The confident speaker's motto is 'practice, practice, practice.' There is no substitute for practice. An old English proverb says *'Speaking without practice is like firing without aiming.'*

Practice takes time and in this time-poor world, we may be enticed to take shortcuts and reduce practice time. Resist the urge. Practice does lead towards perfection and generates the confidence required to deliver successfully.

Follow the inspiring lead of sporting legends like Tiger Woods and Shane Warne who spent many hours practising to perfect their art.

DUNCAN ARMSTRONG'S GOLD MEDAL

At the 1988 Seoul Olympics, Australian swimmer Duncan Armstrong broke the world record to win the gold medal in the 200m freestyle. I remember watching the race on TV with my then girlfriend (who later became my wife). It was a sensational race and as Duncan neared the end we excitedly screamed in unison 'Go Duncan, go Duncan!' And Duncan certainly did go, bringing home gold in record time.

A decade after that win, I had the honour of introducing Duncan as the keynote speaker at a business function. During his motivational presentation on success, Duncan stated *'Success doesn't just happen – you have to work hard for it. My career in swimming taught me that success is a process.'*

He went on to tell us that the process included waking up at 4am each morning, in summer and in winter. Four in the morning … in winter! Each day, every day! He joked that his legendary coach Laurie Lawrence would knock on his door if he wasn't at the pool by a certain time.

Duncan also added that the Australian swimming squad arrived at Seoul early in order to acclimatise to the humid conditions. It gave the Australian swimmers an advantage over their competitors. Duncan and his coach did everything in their power to practise and get ready to win that gold medal. Duncan is living proof that success starts with good processes and practice.

Begin your success as a speaker by adhering to Duncan's advice. Make it a process, practice at every opportunity and you will start to see speaking success.

Communicate Often

Presenting to an audience can be daunting. One way to begin practising your 'conversation' with an audience is to start small. First, develop the art of conversation with one person.

THE JOURNEY OF A THOUSAND MILES BEGINS WITH … A ONE-ON-ONE CONVERSATION

Most of us engage with others numerous times each day. It may be speaking with your children over breakfast, conversing with colleagues at a team meeting or chatting to a friend on the phone.

To assess how well you are conversing with others, ask yourself:

Do I give others my full attention so that they can inform me? Or, do I monopolise the conversation or keep interrupting the other person?

Do I have positive conversations? Or do I engage in gossip and make negative comments?

Do I listen intently so I can understand and empathise with others? Or am I half-attentive and half-focused on what I am going to say next?

READ AND THINK EXTENSIVELY

Sometimes it is difficult to know what to say, particularly to people you have just met. You may feel shy. You may think you have nothing in common. Or you may just feel intimated by someone with higher credentials or a higher profile than you.

To be an interesting speaker, first you need to be an interesting person. One way to become an interesting person is to read.

SUNIL'S AUSTRALIAN INDUCTION

A friend of mine, Sunil, is of Indian decent and had not long been working in Australia. He approached me with a problem that many new migrants face when they first come to Australia for work. How to communicate effectively with Australians? Most people feel quite comfortable conversing with their own community because they have many common threads and topics to discuss. But when they have to communicate with other communities, some people struggle to find common ground.

Sunil was in his early thirties and quite comfortable communicating with his friends. However when he had to talk to people newly introduced to him or even to work colleagues, he got a little tongue-tied and shy.

I suggested using a conversation ice-breaker technique like talking about the weather. He agreed that that was a nice start, but then what?

I asked Sunil what his work colleagues talked about. He said 'Well, they talk about rugby league, but I don't know anything about that sport'.

I suggested to Sunil that he start to learn about rugby league, so at least he could join in the Monday morning conversations. He decided to take my advice and commenced reading the sport pages in the newspaper. He surfed the web to find out more about the game. He even began to follow the Parramatta

Eels because he lived in the area. He learned about the players and watched the games on TV.

On Mondays, he was able to converse with work colleagues about the results of the weekend matches. On Fridays, he was ribbing them about how the Parramatta Eels would win big on the weekend.

Sunil had discovered the secret of how to connect with his work colleagues – find *a mutual topic of conversation.*

But he didn't just stop there. Sunil then started to observe what other topics interested his work colleagues. He researched these new topics, which resulted in him being invited to join them for social events.

This was all because Sunil made the first move to find out what interested others and then made an effort to become an interesting conversationalist on those topics.

We have so much information at our fingertips. The Internet has revolutionised the way we access information. Use this wonderful channel to increase your knowledge on a variety of subjects. Read newspapers. Buy books or borrow them from the library. Digest the information you read. Assess how it can be included in conversations. Develop a voracious appetite for reading.

HOW ONE AVID READER BECAME PUBLIC-SPEAKING WORLD CHAMPION

Jamaican-born Ken Bernard settled in Sydney in the late 1970s. Ken was constantly looking for ways to improve his thinking and his communication. To improve both, Ken joined volunteer organisations that allowed him to explore ideas in meetings and speak at forums.

He listened to motivational speakers' tapes, from Jim Rohn and Brian Tracy to Zig Zigler. Ken was also committed to improving his diction. He spent many hours listening to radio broadcasters and focused intently on how to enunciate certain words. Then Ken would practise these until he spoke like a professional broadcaster.

To further enhance his communication skills, Ken joined Toastmasters International, an organisation committed to improving the public-speaking skills of its members.

While learning the art of communication, Ken decided to challenge himself further. He participated in a number of public-speaking contests and developed his capabilities to such depths that in 1982, Ken Bernard represented Australia in the World Championship of Public Speaking and WON! He became the first Australian to be crowned World Champion.

I once asked Ken to what he attributed his success as a speaker.

'In a word, *reading*. If you want to improve your speaking, first you need to read. Read extensively. Read on a variety of topics. Decide what subject you want to become an authority on and read even more about that subject.

'Reading enables *knowledge*. Knowledge is a powerful thing because through knowledge you gain confidence. When you have confidence in your abilities, you can achieve anything you put your mind to.'

If you want to improve your confidence level, learn from a World Champion. Read, and read extensively. Gain knowledge and increase your self-esteem.

Then go out and *converse*.

A cautionary note ... with all your new-found knowledge on a particular topic, you may feel the urge to share as much of this as you can with others. Resist the urge. A good conversationalist listens more than he speaks. I'm sure you have heard the saying that 'God gave us one mouth and two ears with good reason.' So, listen well and listen often and people will think you are a great conversationalist.

Combat Your Nerves

Most presenters encounter nerves prior to speaking. Some speakers suffer from nerves a few weeks out from the presentation. Other speakers get anxious as speech time looms. This anxiety is sometimes referred to as *performance anxiety*, and it can hinder ultimate performance.

Performance anxiety is often associated with athletes, especially at the top level of sport, where the athlete is competing in front of a large audience or where there is much at stake. But performance anxiety can happen to anyone and in any situation where you are expected to perform to a certain standard. For example, you can experience performance anxiety at work when you are feeling under pressure, or when you are learning the ropes at a new job.

Experiencing performance anxiety is a real possibility for many speakers. It is often said that nerves are good before speech time as it demonstrates that you care about your message and keeps you primed to present. But sometimes the nerves are so bad, they can become a hindrance. If you are really nervous, the best way to overcome performance anxiety is to think positive and to relax your body.

HOW KEN BERNARD DEALT WITH PERFORMANCE ANXIETY

Ken Bernard's world-championship-winning speech was on the topic of *enthusiasm*. I have witnessed Ken re-enact his winning speech many times. As a speaker he has the whole package: wonderful *humour* and *wit*, a *powerful message*, delivered with *tremendous enthusiasm*.

People often ask Ken if he got nervous prior to presenting his speech at the world championship.

'Of course I was nervous. In fact, a few minutes before I had to speak, I was petrified. All types of doubts crept in my mind.

'Was the speech good enough?'

'Would the audience laugh at my jokes? '

'Would I connect with my message?'

'And then my body started to react to these negative thoughts. First, my heart started pounding. I thought I was going to have a heart attack. Then I started to perspire … profusely. Finally, my whole body began to tense up. Now, I was s*cared stiff.*

'I decided that there was only one course of action to get my body to relax.

'I leapt off my chair, got down under the table and rigorously did twenty *push-ups*. Boy did that *rejuvenate* me. The blood was flowing again, the mind started to become positive again. And when it was my turn, I was *ready*. I gave the *performance of my life.'*

Next time you start to get performance anxiety, do some type of physical activity such as deep breathing, or tensing and relaxing parts of your body, or perhaps get down and do some *push-ups*.

THE AUDIENCE IS ON YOUR SIDE

One of the great fears that most new presenters have is *fear* of the audience.

'What will they think of me?'

'What if they don't like me?'

These fears are compounded when the speaker sees people in the audience regard them with a look that seems to say 'prove to me that you are worthwhile'. Some men tend to do this. You see them in the audience and there they are, sitting back in their chairs, arms folded across their chests, giving the speaker 'that look'.

I find that once you have something worthwhile to say, and start to connect with the audience, then these men often change their stance. No more folded arms. They are actually starting to enjoy the presentation.

Remember, however, that most people want you to succeed. If you succeed with your message, your listeners gain too as they derive value. It's a *win-win* situation.

Make sure that you do not misread audience reaction – a mistake I made on the occasion described below.

The Day I Thought I was in Enemy Territory

In 1998, I was invited by Westpac RSL to deliver a short speech for their traditional Anzac Day ceremony. I felt deeply honoured to be invited and gratefully accepted the invitation. To prepare for the speech, I researched heavily at the NSW State Library spending many a lunch hour pouring over the works of official war historian and correspondent Charles Bean. I wanted to make sure that I had all my facts right and that I was fully prepared for this important occasion.

The Westpac RSL ceremony was held the day before Anzac Day and all employees at the main Sydney branch were invited to attend. At the appropriate time, I commenced my short presentation to 40 branch employees. I attempted to make eye contact with people in each section of the audience. Everything was going smoothly until I saw a woman staring at me with what looked like an angry expression. She almost stopped me in my tracks. This woman was probably in her mid-fifties. She was standing slightly away from the others and had her hands folded across her chest. I have to admit that I felt unnerved.

But I composed myself and carried on. I tried to avoid making eye contact with her, but it was a real challenge to ignore a complete section of the audience. So, I sneaked a quick look in her direction. Yes, you guessed it. No change. She was looking right at me, arms folded, with a very serious expression.

I wondered if I had *offended* her in some way. Doubts crept in. After all, here I was, an ethnic Australian, talking about something as sacred as Anzac Day, an occasion where so many Australians gave up their lives for their country.

Soon after my presentation ended, the ceremony concluded with a trumpeter playing the *Last Post*. A number of people came up to speak with me afterwards. I noticed that the serious woman was waiting at the back of the line to speak with me.

Finally, we got to meet.

I wasn't sure what to expect, but what she said completely floored me.

'That was one of the most moving speeches I have ever heard. Thank you for your presentation.'

I was *stunned*. That was the last thing I expected her to say.

So, why did she look so serious? Who knows? Perhaps she was intensely focusing on the message, or simply saddened by the events we were commemorating.

I learnt a valuable lesson that day. The audience is on your side even if it does not look that way.

So, *take heart*. The audience *does* want you to succeed. Feel confident of this and focus on providing *value* to your listeners.

Summary

1. Never wing a speech – outstanding presenters never wing it, so why should you? Prepare well to deliver your message.

2. Practice, practice, practice – there is no substitute for practice. Do it often, do it well and watch your confidence soar.

3. Communicate often – communicate on a one-to-one basis with others to increase your confidence. Read extensively as this will give you more 'speaking' material.

4. Deal with performance anxiety – to build confidence, do some type of physical activity prior to presenting. This will energise and relax you prior to you speaking.

PART TWO
Structure

The right structure for your speech is vital to its success. Get the structure wrong and all the hard work you put into delivery will be in vain. Structuring your message to get it right for the audience is just as important as the delivery.

The Structure part will be presented in the following logical sequence:

Conceptualising the speech

- Determine the purpose of your speech
- Establish your topic

Developing the speech

- Plan your speech
- Build your speech

Getting ready for show time

- Prepare to present

Determine the Purpose of Your Speech

For any speech or presentation, it is vital to have a *definite* purpose. You need to clearly articulate your aim or objective – the reason you are speaking.

In this chapter you will learn how to develop a clear and definite purpose and this will help you develop your message.

Establish Your Topic

The first step is to decide what to speak about. Deciding your topic often poses a challenge for many prospective presenters.

This chapter will guide you on deciding what you should speak about, and more importantly, how to cater for your audience. Find out the seven key factors that your listeners care about to meet their personal needs. Factor these in when deciding on your topic.

Plan Your Speech

A good plan is a necessity for any message you want to deliver and will assist you in your speaking success.

In this chapter you will learn about different presenting styles. You'll also learn how to clearly and logically plan your speech, creating the framework for a clear opening, informative body and compelling close.

Build Your Speech

While planning your speech is creating the framework, building the speech is adding depth to make it informative and compelling.

Learn how to grab an audience's attention from the very start. Just as important, be aware of what kind of openings to avoid. When building the body of your speech understand how to make your key points and arguments. This is an opportunity to elaborate on your message and provide proof and benefits to sell your message. Finally, learn the best ways to close your speech and how to avoid poor closes.

This chapter also provides guidance on the importance of writing out your speech in full and selecting the best words and phrases to increase success.

Prepare to Present

Here we explore the importance of aligning your speech to a time limit. This will help you to be organised and disciplined in your approach.

You will also learn how to use your key learning senses to memorise your speech, a vital component in meeting your speaking objective.

CHAPTER 5

Determine the Purpose of Your Speech

'Our prime purpose in this life is to help others. And if you can't help them, at least don't hurt them.'

DALAI LAMA

This quote by the Dalai Lama should be the frame of reference for any speech. A speaker's purpose should be to provide value to his or her audience: this could enlightening them with information, or inspiring them towards a better life. Having a clear purpose is essential to the speech's success.

What is it that you want your audience to think, feel and act on? The answers will determine your purpose. And when your purpose aligns to what the Dalai Lama so eloquently states, you have the start of a message that provides value to your audience.

Let's consider how the purpose of a speech fits into the broader picture of a good speech.

Foundations of a Good Speech

All good speeches have at their foundation:

- A definite purpose;
- Logical structure;
- Great content.

A clear and *definite purpose* is fundamental as it allows the presenter to develop a focused message.

A good, *logical structure* will enable the audience to more easily grasp the message.

Great content is the key to connecting with your listeners, maintaining their interest and getting them to act.

Who was the last outstanding speaker you heard or saw? Think back to their message.

Did their speech have a definite purpose?

Did you easily understand the flow because the structure was clear and logical?

Did the message incorporate content that kept you captivated?

This chapter focuses on the *purpose* of your message. Later we will cover how to structure messages and how to connect with your audience with great content.

Audience Expectations

For any speaking opportunity it is vital to obtain an understanding of what your audience is expecting. If you do not meet their expectations, then you are potentially wasting everyone's time, and that is a sure-fire way to ruin your credibility as a speaker.

It is imperative that you obtain a view from the organiser or directly from some of your audience prior to your speech as to what their expectations are. Remember that your audience will have varying levels of experience; some members may already have intimate knowledge of your topic while others may be completely unfamiliar with it. You will have to make a decision to whom you are pitching and what value they will obtain from your message.

The Purpose

There are four main purposes for any presentation. These are:

- To inform: an informative message that provides educational value for your audience;

- To entertain: an entertaining message that focuses on pleasing your audience;

- To influence: an influential message that moves your audience to do something different;

- To inspire: an inspirational message that stimulates your audience to greater heights.

We will now consider each purpose in turn.

TO INFORM

People are always seeking knowledge. They may be looking to confirm what they already know, or seeking to obtain further information or new knowledge.

In the business world each day millions of presentations are delivered to communicate information to audiences about a particular topic or subject. Some examples are:

- A work colleague delivering a technical presentation on the general ledger application;

- A newly appointed manager informing her team of the group's restructure;

- A human resources expert explaining the new timesheet process for employees to adopt.

Another type of presenter who communicates to inform is the journalist. A journalist's main job is to inform, whether through covering a specific story or through broadcasting the news.

If your purpose is to inform, you need to determine:

- A clear objective of what content you want to present;

- Your audience's expectations;

- How you will meet those expectations;

- What information you want your audience to walk away with.

TO ENTERTAIN

Some speakers are required to entertain their audiences. This is usually the case in a relaxed setting where the audience is in the mood to be amused, such as at a wedding or other celebration.

Comedians are entertainers; they do this by making their audience laugh. Even if entertaining is not the main purpose of a speech, it should have some element of entertainment value included. For example, a keynote speaker can entertain with a healthy amount of wit, anecdotes and humour blended together for the audience's pleasure.

If your purpose is to entertain, you need to determine:

- The occasion, the setting and the type of audience;

- Your audience's expectations;

- The type of entertainment (jokes, anecdotes, poems, props) you will include to meet those expectations;

- The feeling you want your audience to have at the end of your presentation.

TO INFLUENCE

We are all salespeople. Every day we sell, influence, persuade. We persuade our kids to eat a healthy breakfast. We market ourselves to our managers and customers (read: sell our talents, products, services, achievements). We influence friends to meet at a new café that offers a mouth-watering selection of cakes.

Most presentations include persuasion to one degree or another. Some examples of these are:

- Influencing a business audience to shift to a new way of working;

- Persuading an audience of retirees to rethink how they manage their financial future;

- Selling the benefits of taking on a leadership role for a non-profit organisation.

Speakers who are required to influence are often salespeople, managers and leaders who need to shift an audience's position to meet their business objective.

If your purpose is to influence, you need to determine:

- A clear objective of what you want your audience to think or do;

- A plan for how you will influence your audience;

- Clear thoughts on how to 'clinch the deal'.

To learn about ways to influence your audience, refer to Chapter 21 later in this book.

TO INSPIRE

Inspiring an audience is arguably the most challenging of all purposes. Inspiring an audience means emotionally connecting with its members and lifting them to greater heights.
Some examples of how speakers inspire are:

- A corporate leader inspires employees to improve productivity or to believe in the new company vision;

- A priest inspires parishioners to live a compassionate and charitable life;

- The leader of a country inspires citizens to play their part in controlling climate change;

- A motivational speaker inspires the audience to lead happier and more successful lives.

If your purpose is to inspire, you need to determine:

- A clear objective of what you want your audience to feel and then act on;

- A plan for how you will inspire your audience;

- The key takeaways to help your audience take action;

- Your actions, after your speech, to keep the momentum building.

To learn about ways to inspire your audience, refer to Chapter 24 later in this book.

Summary

1. A clear purpose is fundamental to all good presentations.

2. Every presentation should have at least one of these purposes: to inform; to entertain; to influence; and/or to inspire.

3. Inform your listeners by providing knowledge.

4. Entertain your listeners through messages that focus on pleasing them in some way.

5. Influence your listeners by moving them to do something different.

6. Inspire your listeners by stimulating them to greater heights.

CHAPTER 6

Establish Your Topic

*'Wise men speak because they have
something to say; fools because they
have to say something.'*

PLATO

Now that you are clear on the intention of your message, you need to decide what to speak about. This can be a challenge for many prospective speakers, and so it is where fear and doubt start to creep in.

Will the audience be interested in what I have to say?

*What if my audience knows more about the topic
than I do?*

What if I make an absolute fool of myself?

As a novice speaker, I was often plagued by doubts like these. If

I was asked to present, many a sleepless night was spent asking myself these fear-ridden questions and working myself into a blubbering mess. You may have encountered similar doubts about your ability to deliver a message that your audience values.

So What Do I Talk About?

To make sure that your message provides value to your audience, remember two important points:

- Only speak on topics that you know about;

- Only speak on topics that your audience cares about.

TOPICS THAT YOU KNOW ABOUT

Imagine that your manager approaches you to present to your peers on a topic that you know very little about. Unless you have the time to learn and become knowledgeable on the topic, you are setting yourself up for failure. If you do have the time and it is a topic you are interested in, then by all means learn as much about the topic as you can to ensure that the information you present is of value to the audience.

Make a list of topics that you would be happy to speak about. These may be work related, or topics that could inform, inspire, persuade or entertain an audience. To choose a topic, ensure that:

- You know more about the topic than your prospective audience;

- You can present new or useful information or present in a way that has not been done before.

TOPICS THAT YOUR AUDIENCE CARES ABOUT

What you care about may be vastly different from what your audience cares about. Your audience will always have the *'so what?'* response. This is your audience asking 'How is this message helping me or what I care about?'

Remember that if you do not meet your audience's expectations then you have wasted everyone's time, including your own.

So what does your audience care about? To put it another way, what do they want?

We can never be sure exactly what people want but psychologists believe that most people want:

- To belong;

- To be respected;

- To be liked;

- To be safe;

- To succeed;

- To find love;

- To be inspired.

Have a think about whether these are also your desires. Once you can relate to them on a personal level, then you can better understand what most people subconsciously desire.

When choosing your topic, ensure that your message includes at least one of the elements that people want and you will be well on your way to delivering a message that connects. Once you determine what your specific audience needs, work on your topic to see how your message can fulfil that need in some way.

Here are some considerations to bear in mind when aligning topics to what people want:

To Belong

People want to belong: perhaps to a group of like-minded people or a group who shares the same passion. Or they may have an affinity with a particular lifestyle.

For speaking consider ...

If you are selling luxury cars and your audience is made up of aspirational middle-class people, your sales presentation could aim to get those people to feel that they have (or deserve to have) the lifestyle that includes luxury cars.

To Be Respected

Everyone wants some level of respect and your audience deserves respect.

The best way to show your listeners respect is to understand their specific needs and meet those needs in your message.

For speaking consider ...

If your audience is made up of people wanting basic knowledge on managing their personal finances, pitch your presentation towards the fundamentals so they can learn how to make better financial decisions.

To Be Liked

We all want to be liked. Audience members take great delight in being recognised even for small things. We love hearing our own names or being acknowledged for something. When you are speaking look for opportunities to recognise others.

For speaking consider ...

Use audience member's names whenever possible. Recognise them for their achievements, ideas and actions. Praise people (but be authentic).

To Be Safe

Change is sometimes challenging for people. We are creatures of comfort and anything that challenges that can be met with resistance. Your topic can provide your listeners with reassurance that even though things are changing they will be OK and looked after.

For speaking consider...

You are managing the implementation of a new system. The users who are comfortable with the old system may resist using the new one. Your message should focus on the benefits to them of the new system and importantly show them how easy it is to use (through training and practice). Make them feel safe about using the new system.

To Succeed

Your listeners all want to succeed in some way. Show them the way, make it easier for them by informing them, or influencing them so that they can add another step in their journey to personal success.

For speaking consider ...

Visualise yourself speaking to a group of high school students who need to manage their time better to cope with homework, exams and life. Make them understand how goal setting and time management will help them take control of their lives.

To Find Love

Most people want to be loved, whether it's by family, friends or romantic love. This is quite a specific need and unless you are qualified or have a special interest in this area then you may need to take a creative approach to the topic.

For speaking consider ...

Giving an inspirational speech urging people to care for others, such as by volunteering. This perhaps could lead to their receiving gratitude, respect and even love from the people they have helped. Consider whether this could be a side benefit to the course of action being proposed.

To Be Inspired

People want inspiration in their lives. We need heroes or, better still, to be the heroes.

Inspire your audience to greater heights. If you can do this, then you are well on your way to becoming a great presenter.

For speaking consider ...

You are in a leadership position and want to inspire your team to improve results. Helping your listeners visualise a better future and informing them of their part in making that future materialise will inspire them into action.

Summary

1. When you are thinking about your topic, ensure (a) you only speak on topics that you know about, and (b) you only speak on topics that your audience cares about.

2. Your audience wants to belong. Help your audience to have a sense of belonging or affinity to the topic of your speech.

3. Your audience wants to be respected: respect your audience by understanding and meeting their specific needs.

4. Your audience wants to be liked: recognise and acknowledge specific members of your audience during your presentation.

5. Your audience wants to be safe: help your audience to overcome resistance to change by demonstrating benefits and making it easier to adopt change.

6. Your audience wants to succeed: influence and inspire your audience to take steps towards achieving personal success.

7. Your audience wants to find love: (only if you are appropriately knowledgeable) guide your audience to find love or romance.

8. Your audience wants to be inspired: inspire your audience to do something differently to meet a particular need or cause.

CHAPTER 7

Plan Your Speech

*'By failing to prepare,
you are preparing to fail.'*

Benjamin Franklin

There is only one way to give a great speech and that is to have a good plan. If you are like most of us, you are probably groaning at the very thought of developing a plan. Why not dive into writing the speech and let it shape up as time goes by? Resist this thought as you guiltily cast your eye back to the Benjamin Franklin quote above.

Take the time to develop a good speech plan, and you will reap the benefit of your efforts many times over.

The purpose of planning a speech is to confirm your message, know what you should convey and importantly what should be omitted from your speech. Don't be the best man who neglects to thank the bridesmaids, the MC who forgets the keynote speaker's name or the speaker who babbles on for eons without making a meaningful point. A good plan will also inject confidence into your presentation.

When you are planning your speech, focus on these two key aspects:

- Your speaking style;

- How you structure the message.

Speaking Style

Your style of speaking will depend on the audience and the occasion. When you are developing the content for a speech it is important to know how you will address your audience. Will it be very formal or will you speak casually? Or will it be a combination of formal and informal?

If you were addressing dignitaries at an important conference, you would probably present in a formal manner. If you were raising the toast at a wedding among family and friends you would, given the joyous occasion, present in an informal manner.

Here are five language registers to consider when matching your presentation style to the occasion and your audience's expectations.

FROZEN

Frozen language is prescribed language that does not change. These are 'set' speeches, often scripted. An example is a prayer during a Mass at church: 'I offer my prayers to God'.

FORMAL

Formal language makes use of complete sentences and specific words. Think of a formal setting such as a parliamentary session or when making an official complaint: 'Your service was less than satisfactory. I demand a refund'.

CONSULTATIVE

This language is used with colleagues and peers, perhaps at a meeting: 'As discussed, let's now confirm actions on how to resolve the supplier crisis'.

CASUAL

This type of informal language would be used in conversation with friends or family: 'Hey mate, what's up?'

INTIMATE

This is language between lovers or good friends, often containing 'private' terms: 'How are you, honey-bun?'

For the purpose of most business presentations, the appropriate style will be in the 'consultative' and 'casual' range, and adopt a *conversational tone*.

Growing up as a good practising Catholic, I remember the days when sermons at Mass were of the 'fire and brimstone' variety. These sermons were designed to scare the living daylights out of you and inspire you to obey the Church's rules or forever be damned. But those days are long gone. No-one likes to be preached at. Audiences today want to be engaged and listen to a speaker who is prepared to have a conversation with them. A conversational speaker uses vocal dynamics that are similar to ordinary conversation, but adapted to the environment and audience to which the speech is being delivered.

US President Barack Obama is a master at speaking with a conversational style and he employed this to great advantage in his 'chats' with the American people. He connected with his fellow Americans during racially motivated incidents by changing the focus from race to being decent human beings. At times he connected with Americans from the standpoint of a normal parent, facing the same concerns as they would for their children.

A good tip for writing your message is to *write as if you are having a conversation with someone specific.*

Purpose

Determine the purpose of your speech, as discussed in Chapter 5, and keep it in mind as you plan you speech. Let's say that you want to present an idea to influence an audience. If your purpose is to influence, you would:

- Provide factual, accurate and sufficient information;

- Overcome the audience's objections;

- Create action or acceptance of your ideas;

- Lay the foundation to build stronger relationships with your audience.

Structure

A clear and logical structure will help your audience to easily grasp the point of your presentation and the message you want to convey.

The simplest way to develop structure is to use the following format:

Opening > Body > Close.

Let's look at each of these important segments to help you plan your message.

OPENING

The three main goals to achieve in your opening are:

- Connect immediately with your audience;

- Introduce your topic and agenda;

- Establish your credibility.

Connect Immediately With Your Audience

Why should your audience listen to you? Generally speaking, people today have short attention spans. If you do not connect with them instantly and keep them connected, you'll see them reaching for their mobile phones and playing with them instead of listening to you. Your main objective in the precious opening moments is to capture your audience's attention.

How will you do this? A short, sharp anecdote? A witty quote? A startling fact? A joke (fraught with danger unless you are confident that this will work)?

Think about what will immediately get your audience to sit up, take note and look forward with anticipation to the rest of the speech. Further information and examples are covered in the following Build Your Speech chapter.

Introduce Your Topic and Agenda

Start by establishing what you will be speaking about and provide your audience with an outline of your message.

While working for a major bank, I invited an executive to speak about agile methodology to a group of organisational change managers. Unfortunately the executive used the first few minutes to provide a ton of background information rather than introducing his topic. I felt the audience was getting confused as to the exact point of his message and would have reached for their mobile phones if he were not an executive.

It is vital to come straight to the point in your opening gambit: explain what it is you will be talking about and provide your audience with a roadmap of what you will be covering.

Establish Your Credibility

Your audience members are asking themselves 'who is this person who is going to take up the next 30 minutes of my life while I listen to them?'

Again it is important that this is answered. It's best to have an MC introduce you with sufficient information to answer the audience's question. If there is no MC, then establish credibility yourself when you start to speak.

Your credibility can be demonstrated in various ways, such as describing your experience, standing in business, expertise, qualifications or anything that will get the audience to believe that you can speak with authority on the topic.

BODY

The main goals to achieve with the body of your message are:

- Outline the problem or situation;
- Present key points and supporting evidence for each point or idea.

Outline the Problem or Situation

A good way to start addressing your topic is to describe the current problem or situation that you intend to change.

For example, if speaking to teenagers about driving safely, you might outline the current state of affairs by pointing to the large number of deaths or injuries caused by reckless teenage driving. You are setting the scene by outlining the problem we face today and the consequences it has.

Present Key Points and Support Each Idea

Audiences are looking for a 'headline', a way to position your idea in their own minds. So, create a one-line description for each of your ideas, so that you can help your listeners mentally categorise them. Provide them with the big picture (one-line description) first before filling in the details.

Once you have outlined the situation or problem, you now need to provide the solution. Going back to our previous example, the solution might be: teenagers need to take more precautions when driving and a good beginning is to adhere to speed limits.

Your solution then needs to be backed up and supported accordingly.

The PRES Principle

A principle I like to use when thinking about how to present is the PRES principle. PRES stands for:

Point

Reason

Example

Summary

The PRES principle can be used as such: make a Point > support it with a Reason > support the reason with an Example > provide a Summary

Here is how it would be applied to our reckless driving example:

(Make a Point) One way to improve safety when driving is to turn off your mobile phone.

(Point supported by Reason) Mobile phones are now considered one of the main reasons why teenagers get distracted when driving, either by texting or speaking on the phone.

(Reason supported by an Example) Recently a teenager in my local area admitted he was texting on the phone while speeding. He lost control of his car and went through a neighbour's fence, ending up in their pool. No-one was hurt, but they could have been. Imagine the consequences if there had been children swimming in the pool at that time.

(Summary) Please be aware that mobile phones are distractions and can cause accident, injury or death to yourselves and others. Make a commitment to stop using your mobile phone while driving.

Make three main points in the body of your message following the formula above and you have the makings of a good speech.

CLOSE

The all-important close is your opportunity to tie up all of the key points you have made into a summary. This is also the opportunity to drive home your message, get the audience to act on it and leave them wanting more.

The main goals to achieve in the close are:

- Summarise your message;
- Provide a call to action;
- Leave a lasting impression.

Summarise Your Message

The close is where you bring it all together. Start with a summary of the main points that you have made.

Using the example above of speaking to teenagers about safety while driving, you could summarise by saying 'Today, I have covered some key points to help you to drive more safely on the roads. The three main points I have made were to eliminate distractions like using mobile phones, always be conscious of keeping to the speed limit, and be aware of what's happening around you.'

Call to Action

The summary should lead to a *call to action* for your audience. The call to action is asking your audience to consider the points you have made and take some type of action.

In this example, the call to action might be 'When driving, always think safety first. Thinking safety first will lead you to drive more safely on the roads and protect yourself, your passengers and other people. Please respect yourself, respect others and respect the law. Be safe.'

Leave a Lasting Impression

This is your final opportunity to really connect with your audience. Plan to include something that will leave your audience inspired, keen to hear you speak again or thinking how memorable your speech was. We will discuss this in greater depth in the next chapter, Build your Speech.

Summary

A good speech needs a good plan. Remember the following:

1. Decide the style of speaking you will use. This will depend on the occasion, the audience and their expectations of your message.

2. Where possible, always use a conversational style rather than a 'preacher' style. Having a conversation will help you better connect with your audience.

3. Create a clear and logical structure for your presentation that includes an opening, body and close.

4. Ensure that your opening connects

immediately with the audience, introduces your topic and establishes your credibility.

5. Plan to have the body of your message outline the problem or situation and present key points and support for each idea.

6. When you present each key point, use the PRES formula (make a *point*, supported with a *reason*, supported with an *example* and *summarised*).

7. And finally, plan a great close by summarising your message, having a call to action for your audience and leaving a lasting impression.

CHAPTER 8

Build Your Speech

'Whatever good things we build
end up building us.'

Jim Rohn

The next step after planning your message is to build the speech. This is where you put meat on the bones. Similar to the plan of your speech, a typical build will have an opening, followed by the main body of the speech and finally the conclusion of your message. Let's review each of these key phases from the opening stanza through to the end of the speech.

Fleshing Out Your Structure

OPENING

The first goal of your opening is to connect with your audience. If you do this then you can maintain momentum and deliver a great presentation. Your objective should be to arouse curiosity and interest instantly so that your audience wants to know more.

Let's consider five ways you might achieve this:

1. Ask a Startling Question

By asking a question, you instantly involve your listeners as they contemplate a response. Asking a startling question will get your audience wondering where that came from and it should immediately hook them in.

For example you could ask them *'Have you ever been accused of murder?'*

This could begin a speech on botching a business or investment, not actually murdering a person.

Or you can ask the audience *'Shall you be saved?'*

While this may conjure images of damnation and eternal salvation, it could simply be a speech on how to survive a personal crisis.

2. Provide a Quotation

An effective way to connect with your audience is to lead with a quote. A good quote from a credible source can trigger many responses: from provoking thought to entertaining to inspiring the audience. The quote provides a jumping-off point for your main message.

For example, if your speech is about taking control of your life immediately, you could use this Chinese proverb: *'The best time to plant a tree was 20 years ago. The second best time is now.'*

3. Start with an Illustration or Story

You could start with a short story that sets the scene for the rest of speech. Stories, and especially personal stories, are a magnet for the audience's attention. Telling a great story will help you quickly connect with the audience. For more information on how to develop stories, refer to Chapter 10.

4. Use an Exhibit

An effective way to engage is to exhibit something that the audience can see for themselves. It is even better if they can touch or feel the exhibit to provide an added dimension.

For example, if you are doing a speech on travelling to amazing places, you could show a mobile phone app that has a map of Istanbul in Turkey and point out the historic places to visit, or take a large wall map of Istanbul and invite the audience to gather around for a close-up and personal view.

5. Make a Provocative Statement Related to the Speech Topic

You could even start by making a provocative statement that arouses curiosity, such as 'Look at the person on either side of you. One of you is a bigot.'

Make sure that this is related to the topic and not a random statement.

OPENINGS TO AVOID

Apologetic Statement

'This subject may be a bit dry for some of you.'

General Statement Presented in a General Way
'Most people drive too fast'.

Platitude
'It is indeed a great honour to be here tonight'.

A Story or Joke That Does Not Relate to the Speech Topic
'Two Irishmen went to a pub …' (A joke in an attempt to break the ice, rather than related to the topic. Resist the urge).

BODY
In the body of your message, you need to make your key points or arguments. This is an opportunity to elaborate by providing proof, ideas or benefits to sell your message.

In the previous chapter on planning, you were introduced to the PRES formula: make a Point; support it with a Reason; support the reason with an Example, and then Summarise.

Let's now see how we can build on the PRES formula. Say you are constructing a speech on travel to Singapore. You want to provide the audience with information about three things of interest:

- What to see;

- What to eat and drink;

- What to be aware of.

In considering 'What to see', you might say:

(Point) Singapore is a wonderful place to visit and has many highlights for you to see and do. Singapore has something for everyone. But since you are interested in culture **(Reason)** I would strongly recommend visiting the Singapore Botanical Garden and also the Night Safari.

(Example) A few years ago I visited both these beautiful sites. The Botanical Gardens is a lush oasis, home to stunning flora and fauna and has been honoured as a UNESCO World Heritage site. I spent a whole day there and here are some beautiful photographs **(show them)** I'd like to share.

(Next example) As for the Night Safari, it is a world first in terms of allowing visitors to see over 2500 nocturnal animals in their natural night-time habitats. The amazing guided tram ride takes you across seven geographical zones of the world, from the rugged Himalayan Foothills to the swampy banks of the Asian Riverine Forest. The guide shares fascinating facts and tales about the animals and their habitats.

(Summary) Singapore is a truly wonderful place to take your family on a cultural holiday. Enjoy the diverse activities and sites. Now let me talk about what to eat and drink in Singapore …

Use the PRES formula builds points on 'what to eat and drink' and finally 'what to be 'aware of'.

Provide Facts

There is nothing more compelling than hard facts. Everyone has an opinion and opinions are generally subjective. If you are providing facts make sure that they are accurate or you will lose credibility. It is respectful to attribute the facts to the source. If your facts and sources are credible, then your audience will see you as being credible.

For example, if you are talking about assessing blood alcohol levels, you could say 'According to the New South Wales authority on safer driving, the NRMA Motoring Services:

"Your blood alcohol content, also known as BAC, will begin to rise as soon as you start drinking and usually reach its maximum 20-60 minutes after you stop drinking. There is no quick way to reduce your BAC after you've stopped drinking. Remedies such as exercise, drinking coffee or water or taking a cold shower won't lower your BAC. Time is the only way to clear alcohol from the bloodstream. It can take at least one hour for the body to metabolise each drink you have – it also depends on the alcohol level in each drink. Therefore, make sure enough time has passed before you drive."'

This is great advice for your audience, supported by facts from a credible source.

Keep it Simple

Even the most complex scientific theories can be explained to someone who has little understanding of science as long as they are provided with a *frame of reference*. You don't have to be a rocket scientist to understand the physics involved in going to the moon. It just needs to be presented in a way that the listener can understand. With a few simple techniques, you can describe pretty much anything, and in doing so keep audience members interested and entertained as they learn.

Making comparisons is an effective method. This technique is particularly useful when explaining technical or complex information. Follow these rules to ensure the audience easily grasps what you are attempting to convey:

- Define any words that are not part of ordinary speech;

- Provide a glossary if the topic is very detailed and uses many scientific terms;

- Give simple, step-by-step explanations;

- Provide an example or analogy to support your explanation;

- Use visual aids, such as photos, illustrations and three-dimensional models to reinforce your explanation. It's easier to understand a solar eclipse, for example, if you use round objects and a torch to demonstrate the orbits of the earth and moon and how the moon casts a shadow on the earth.

CLOSE

You want your audience to remember both your message and you. What you say last will be what your audience will remember the most. Here are some thoughts on how to close in a way that's memorable.

Appeal for Definite Action and Set a Deadline

'We can solve this problem if we all take *collective action*. I urge you to write to the councillors by the *end of this week.'* *(Hand out a template letter).*

Tell a Story

You can close by telling a story that captures the essence of your message and if the audience gets the story, they will get your message. A great story will help leave a lasting impression with your audience.

Provide a Quotation

Add depth to your supporting argument by including a great quote that is pertinent to the point you are making.

For example, if you are planning an inspirational speech on perseverance, you could use this quote from Thomas A. Edison: *'Our greatest weakness lies in giving up. The most certain way to succeed is always to try just one more time.'*

CLOSINGS TO AVOID

Inviting the Audience to Ask Questions

You want to end on a high. So once you have finished, wait for the well-deserved applause and then let the MC manage the Q&A.

Pointless Statement

'It was such a pleasure to present to you this evening.'

Apologetic Statement

'I'm sorry that we ran out of time and I was unable to cover everything.'

Thank the Audience

Your listeners should be the ones thanking you for sharing information with them.

Write Out Your Speech in Full

It intrigues me when some people who attend corporate meetings do not take any type of notes. Often these are the same people who do not remember their action points from the meeting. One of my favourite management quotes is *'if it's not written down, it doesn't exist.'* Writing things down enables commitment, whether it is writing down action items, writing objectives or even penning your goals.

The same is true for writing your speech in its entirety. One of the most frequent questions I get asked is 'Do I *have* to write out my speech in full?' Often speakers state that they have a general idea of what they are going to say, that the message is all in their head, or that they have jotted down some bullet points and that should suffice. My strong recommendation is that a presenter should write their speech out in its entirety. It demonstrates that you are serious about your message and are making a commitment to getting it right.

Writing out your full speech has considerable benefits. It helps you to:

- Select the best words or phrases;
- Select words or phrases to emphasise;
- Align the speech to a time limit;
- Memorise your speech through key learning senses.

SELECT THE BEST WORDS OR PHRASES

I have always loved competition, whether it was at sport, or school or public speaking contests. As a youngster, I enjoyed playing board games with my maternal grandmother. My grandmother and I had a special bond and she would teach me many things like the fundamentals of cooking and how to win at board games. Our favourite board game was the word game Scrabble. If you have played Scrabble, you will know that you need to maximise your points by using high-value letters and well-placed words. The game of Scrabble has an element of luck in terms of the letters you get. But the game can also be very strategic as you use the board to look at the best options for your words.

My grandmother taught me one important lesson that helped to improve my Scrabble success. It was this piece of *wisdom:* never ever put down the first word that comes to you. There will always be a better word. Think of all possible options (within your time limit) and come up with the one that gives you the most points or provides a strategic advantage.

With this advice, I was able to get more seven-letter words (along with a 50-point bonus) than many of my opponents. I would look for every opportunity to get those bonus points and the more I looked, the more I got. The ultimate test of skill was playing against my own mother, who had learnt the same tactics from her mother. Coming second to your mum, most of the time, is not such a bad thing.

The relevant point to remember here is that there is often a better word or phrase that you can employ when drafting your presentation. So, it's best to write out your speech in full and then wordsmith it to find more effective words or phrases that will leave your audience appreciating your memorable message.

SELECT WORDS OR PHRASES TO EMPHASISE

Once your speech is written, the use of emphasis on certain words or phrases can really *liven* it up. If it's not written down, you may not remember where to place the emphasis and your opportunity to deliver a strong speech may be *diluted*. The best way to know where to use emphasis is to go through your written speech with a fine-tooth comb, read it out aloud and look for where you need to place emphasis. It's the same process that stand-up comedians use with their punchlines. They set up the joke and punch out the punchline. It's the word or phrase they emphasise that delivers the big impact and the outcome is great laughs. Get the emphasis wrong in the punchline and the joke falls flat.

So, think about where in your speech you can get the *best punch*, or ask for feedback on this from someone you trust. Underline (or bold) the words that you want to emphasise and play around with the emphasis on different words until you work out what will give you the best reaction. All of this takes time, but then nothing good came out of taking the easy road. The more you work at this, the quicker and more adept you will become at selecting words that have maximum impact.

Summary

Build onto your structure of opening, body and close.

Open – your aim is to grab the audience's attention immediately. You can open your message through one of the following ways:

1. Ask a startling question.

2. Provide a quotation.

3. Tell a story or anecdote – personal ones are best.

4. Use an exhibit.

5. Make a provocative statement related to the speech topic.

Body – your objective is to provide the audience with information to build your argument. This is the main meal for the audience. Consider using the following:

1. Provide facts that add weight to your

message. Facts are compelling and add credibility.

2. Keep it Simple – provide your listeners with a frame of reference, something that they can compare to what they already know.

Close – this is the time to leave a lasting impression. Consider the following to close with:

1. A definite action and deadline – be specific as to what you want your audience to do, think or feel and give them a deadline.

2. A memorable story that suits the message and rams home your main point.

3. A great quote or thought that leaves the audience contemplating on your message.

Write out your speech in full, so that you can:

1. Select the best words or phrases.

2. Know the words or key phrases to emphasise.

CHAPTER 9

Prepare to Present

*'Only the prepared speaker
deserves to be confident.'*

DALE CARNEGIE

When you are preparing to present there are some key elements to consider. Incorporating these will help to improve your chances of success when you present your speech.

Align the Speech to a Time Limit

If your speech is not written down, how do you know if you will meet your time obligations? Most presentations have a time limit. You may be part of a series of presentations or a meeting agenda, or even a solo presenter. In all cases you should confirm your allotted time with the meeting coordinator.

I am amazed at the number of presenters who speak over their allotted time. Either they have not practised their presentation with a stop-watch or have guesstimated their time. Regardless, I think that this is disrespectful to the audience, the event host and the speakers who follow, who then have to pay the price by compacting their speaking times.

BREAKING THE TIME LIMIT RULES

Recently, a well-known professional presenter from a speakers bureau was asked to attend a public-speaking award ceremony. The presenter was the guest of honour and his sole duty was to present the key award to a recipient. Following the presentation of the award, the presenter decided to take the opportunity to speak to the 200-strong audience on a range of random topics. The speaker talked for 45 minutes, not heeding clues from many of the audience who walked out of the room. Just as it was getting embarrassing, the host finally got up and informed the guest of honour that there were other conference events that the audience had to attend. The professional speaker then took the liberty of a few more minutes to finish his talk.

Who was to blame for this debacle? Both the event coordinator and the professional speaker must accept responsibility. The event coordinator's role is to ensure that the program speakers keep to their allocated time. The speaker should manage their time allocation and respectfully keep to this. Speakers and event coordinators should always aim to respect their host and the audience.

I know that the public-speaking organisation will not repeat this embarrassment. You will do irreparable damage to your reputation if you commit the cardinal sin of not respecting and keeping to your time limit. Always ensure that you know your speaking time limit and respect the time expectations if you want to be a repeat client or a well-respected speaker.

Memorise Your Speech through Key Learning Senses

If you want to appear credible and confident as a speaker, you need to memorise your speech and convey your message directly to the audience.

Here is a simple but powerful technique for memorising your speech. Utilise your two main learning senses, visual and auditory, by seeing the words of your speech on paper and then reading them aloud.

Split the speech into four or five sections, then read the first section out aloud a few times. After a while you should be able to memorise that section. Without referring to your written notes, try to verbalise that section. You may make some errors or not recall some words at which point you can refer back to the written speech. Once you have conquered memorising section one, move onto the next section. Then recite section one and two together. And so on. The time will be well spent and greatly enhance credibility with your audience.

Summary

1. Align your speech to a time limit – this helps you to be organised and is respectful to your audience.

2. Memorise your message by using your key learning senses: visual and auditory.

PART THREE
Connect

During a consulting assignment I approached a senior manager requesting the support of someone from his team, a person who could act as an advocate for the change I was managing. I explained to the manager that a suitable candidate should be well respected by peers, a good communicator and able to influence others to embrace the change.

He simply said 'Go down to the local pub on a Friday evening after work. 'I replied 'I'd be happy to.' (I love a drink as much as the next person). 'Any particular reason?'

He replied 'When you're at the pub, check out the person who is *holding court*. There's always one person whom everyone else is crowded around, eagerly listening to their banter and joining in the fun.'

I decided to follow his sage advice. Sure enough there was one individual holding court. I later met with 'the man' and he agreed to support me on my mission. He was an excellent choice and with his great ability to connect with others, made the change a lot easier to sell to others.

Do you know someone who has this ability? I'm sure you do. Observe them closely. Why do people flock to them as bees to honey? What makes them so special? What secret talent do they have to attract others?

Many years ago at a work Christmas party, I observed another one of these special people whom everyone veered to like a magnet. He waltzed into the party late, and was decked out in black leather pants and top (outlandish in those days). In his hand he held a gold sceptre that he kept slowly twirling around.

I don't know whether the glittering sceptre played any part in it, but it was his charismatic personality that led many of the women in the room to flock over to him. This gentleman had a great sense of fun about him. From a distance I observed him telling anecdotes and jokes that kept his audience enthralled.

Wow! If only that kind of talent could be bottled and marketed. I'm sure if it were, most of us would be lining up to buy it.

Connecting with others, either one-on-one, within a team or with an audience, is one of the great keys to success. We can connect on many levels; through shared experiences, through laughter, even with a simple smile.

In this part we look at some of the ways to connect with others, as an individual having a conversation with another person or as a speaker who wants to hold court with an audience.

The connect part includes the following chapters:

Tell Stories

People tell stories every single day. As a speaker, telling stories that grab the attention of your audience is essential to how you influence them.

In this chapter you will learn the key elements of good storytelling, when to include a story and how best to introduce a story into your presentation. You will also learn where to find good stories and how to bring you story alive for your audience.

Use Humour

One of the most effective ways to connect with others is through humour: a quip, a funny story, a good pun or a bit of banter.

This chapter will focus on what kind of humour is relevant. You will learn the importance of self-effacing humour and, most importantly, how to use humour effectively in your speech.

Speak with Passion

Presenters who speak passionately resonate with their audience. Sharing a message with passion will help a speaker instantly connect.

This chapter helps you to discover your passion, prepare to share that passion and deliver to exceed your audience's expectations.

Show Vulnerability

Sharing your weakness in this competitive world is akin to committing hara-kiri. Or is it? Displaying vulnerability, putting our faults on display, proves that we are human. This can be a powerful way to connect with others through creating empathy.

You will learn how to be vulnerable in your daily interactions with others and how to show vulnerability when you present to others. This is a powerful chapter that can alter the way you see your life and how you interact with others.

Use Powerful Body Language

A vital part of your impact as a person of influence and as a speaker depends upon your body language. Using the right body language can really help you connect with your audience.

You will learn how to be aware of negative body language and how to avoid this when speaking to an audience. You will also learn how to use powerful physical gestures to support your message. In addition you will come to understand the importance of using facial expressions to convey six strong emotions: these are factors to consider especially when you are telling a story or making an emotional appeal.

Cultivate Charisma

Most people find it difficult to articulate what charisma is. They can tell you *who* they think is charismatic, but may not be able to tell you what characteristics form that charisma.

This chapter looks at the six traits that charismatic people have as defined by Ronald E. Riggio. We will consider how you can use your natural charisma, develop traits to become more charismatic, and explore how to use these traits when you are speaking to an audience.

Care for Your Audience

This is one of the most important ways to really connect with your audience. Care for others is a gift that each of us can choose to possess.

This chapter focuses on how you care for the most important people when speaking: your audience. It is divided into two sections: how to respect your audience before, during and after the speech; and how to develop compassion for others.

All seven chapters in the Connect part are designed so that you can immediately take the concepts into practice, start to connect with others and observe how your relationships transform for the better. Connect now!

CHAPTER 10

Tell Stories

*'There is no greater agony than
bearing an untold story inside you.'*

MAYA ANGELOU

Humans are natural storytellers. We have been telling stories since the dawn of time. Think of cave drawings. Those were stories created by a civilisation and told lovingly to each forthcoming generation.

We tell stories every day ... around the water cooler at work, when sharing a meal with friends, when relaxing in the evening with family. Anecdotes like how some idiot driver on the road cut you off this morning, or the argument you observed between two teenage girls on the bus. We tell stories all the time without even being aware that we are doing it.

Childhood Memories

One of my fondest memories is of my mother telling us stories at bedtime when I was a young boy. She concocted stories about the adventures of two crabs, Colin and Carpy. Years later, I still recall those stories with the same warmth, fondness and affection as when they were being lovingly told by her. I'm sure you remember your own childhood when perhaps your parents read to you or told you stories about elves, fairies, princesses, kings or animals and their adventures. My belief is that no matter what our age, nothing grabs our attention more than a good story. People love to listen to a story and the better narrated it is the more interest there is from the listener. Books of fiction are of course one long story and are extremely popular, as they momentarily transport us away from our daily problems and challenges.

Do you tell stories? Do you invent stories for your children? Do you include stories when you present to others? Telling stories adds a wonderful dimension to the way we converse with others. Think of the anecdotes you tell work colleagues on Monday mornings about the highlights from your weekend. Or when you inform your partner about how your day was ruined because of an altercation you had with a colleague.

A story can be defined as a narrative, either true or fictitious, designed to interest, amuse, or instruct the listener or reader. Stories may inspire, thrill or sadden us. A good story should evoke an emotional response that will resonate with the reader, viewer or listener.

What Makes a Good Story?

We've all experienced *bad* storytelling: the boring movie that made your mind wander; the book you picked up multiple times but just never got into; that certain in-law who always stuffs up the punchline to the joke; and the friend who's always going off on tangents confusing all of his intended listeners. These instances make us roll our eyes, or take our minds elsewhere, perhaps contemplating what we'll have for dinner later.

But we've also experienced *good* storytelling: the novel that kept you up all night because you couldn't wait to find out what happened next; the movie you saw three times and then bought on DVD; and the grandfather who makes up outlandish and wonderful bedtime stories off the top of his head. These stories captivate us and hold our interest, we can't tear ourselves away and we lose track of the outside world. We are enchanted and enthralled.

ELEMENTS OF GOOD STORYTELLING

For inclusion in a speech, the elements of good storytelling are:

- Establishing the situation quickly;

- Bringing emotion to your story;

- Being creative and building pictures;

- Bringing it all together at the end.

Establish the Situation Quickly

You will lose your audience if it takes too long to get to the point. Establish the situation within the first couple of minutes. The challenge is to grab the audience's attention and keep it.

For example I can start off with this statement: 'Three hundred people in your local community die unnecessarily each year!'

To establish the situation quickly, here is how I might follow-up on that attention-grabbing statement: 'Let me share with you a story about Ron, who was part of my local community.

Ron was my next-door neighbour and friend and we were close. I remember Ron and I used to walk to school together, except Ron used a walking stick. You see, Ron used this stick because he was morbidly obese. Ron was only thirteen years old.'

Bring Emotion into Your Story

The story must be narrated with the appropriate emotion and drama. If the storyteller drones on in a monotone, most of the impact of the story will be lost. Voice modulation with the right pitch and pauses is the key to evoking emotion. The effective use of pauses can make your audience hang on every word with anticipation and excitement. In the following example, italics have been used to show where emphasis could be placed.

'Imagine life as a thirteen year old, being morbidly obese and using a walking stick to support you. You couldn't run around and play with the other kids (pause). Most kids would poke fun at you, because kids can be *very cruel* (pause). I remember Ron being *really upset* at cruel taunts which made him *sob uncontrollably* at times. Was it Ron's *fault* that he was morbidly obese? (pause) *Somewhat!* His parents were divorced and he was being raised by a single mother who worked most days to support them. His father leaving them *upset him greatly* and he found *solace* in food; fast food and lots of it. A lack of exercise and junk food were *recipes* for Ron's obesity.'

Be Creative

Telling the right story to the right audience at the right moment is vital. Plan your presentation and design the story creatively to drive home the message. Build pictures in the audience's mind.

Good storytelling is often the difference between a good presenter and an average one. Excellent presenters take the time to plan their stories and weave them perfectly into their overall presentation. A good creative story that is told with word pictures will ensure the audience is engaged, interested and ideally captivated. Word pictures are visuals or pictures conjured in the listener's mind as the speaker is describing something.

'Ron became more obese over time right before my eyes. It was like watching someone build a snowman – adding more snow to the face, patting layers of snow around the body and building a big base at the bottom.

This was Ron. He was like an automatic garbage disposal unit, shovelling the worst kinds of food into his body. Each day he swallowed the equivalent of ten cups of refined sugar, two litres of oil and fat and five cups of salt. If I blended those ingredients together, it would look pretty disgusting. More than disgusting, it was really sad.

One bright sunny day, the dark clouds rolled into Ron's world. He had a heart attack at fourteen. The good news was that the operation was a success. The great news was that, just like a loud alarm rudely wakes us up in the morning, it was Ron's wake-up call!'

Bring It All Together

The closing is key to delivering impact. It is your opportunity to ensure the audience is clear about the moral of the story. You may choose to end the story dramatically, leaving the audience to come to their own conclusion. The best way to close is with a bit of mystery or a one-line explanation that leaves the lessons to sink in.

'Ron's path to recovery was painfully slow. He had to undo all the self-inflicted damage. But he had the wonderful support of doctors, his mum and friends. He went on a healthy diet, started to exercise with me every day and even started yoga classes. It took three long years, but I'm proud to report that Ron lost 80kgs and is now a fit man with a beautiful family.

Obesity is a problem in this country. But when you look at Ron's story there is a rainbow. There is a way to beat obesity. If you know of anyone suffering from this disease, be kind to them – be their wake-up call.'

NARRATING A GOOD STORY

My wife, Gayle, is a good storyteller. She establishes the situation quickly, takes her audience on the journey and builds the story to a climax.

At a recent lunch with friends, we were about to relate an incident where our flight was diverted to St. Petersburg due to a medical emergency. We thought it would be great for our teenage son to tell the story as he was closest to what eventuated during the medical episode. Rather than setting up the story, he jumped straight into 'A lady had a heart attack …' So, his mother took over to explain the episode in greater detail.

Gayle started off with 'On our flight from Hong Kong to London, we visited St. Petersburg, which was an unscheduled stop.' See how her story begins with an immediate hook **(attention-grabbing opening)** that arouses the curiosity of her listeners.

Once Gayle had her audience's attention, she explained how we were situated on the plane three rows from where the drama unfolded. It was near the exit doors that a female passenger collapsed with a suspected heart attack *(establishing the situation quickly)*.

She described how the airline staff responded by working on the passenger for hours, detailed how we landed on a non-commercial air-strip, and what happened when the Russian service personnel came on board.

Gayle shared our feelings about the wellbeing of the passenger, hoping that she was OK, particularly during the three times the defibrillator was used and each time we thought that the passenger was not going to make it *(bringing emotions to the story)*.

The landing of the plane proved dramatic with the crew unable to secure themselves with seat belts as they needed to tend to the passenger. There were many courageous people that night ensuring that the sick passenger was their only priority.

Gayle added much more detail than I have provided here to bring colour and depth to the story and evoke the appropriate emotional response *(being creative, building word pictures)*.

Gayle ended the story by describing how after a lengthy wait we took off for our original destination and heard the news that everyone had hoped for. The captain announced that the ill passenger was on the way to recovery in the hospital *(bringing it all together)*.

Our friends enjoyed the whole story rather than my son's very short version. I'm sure he took a few pointers on how to tell good stories from his mother.

Storytelling as a Speaker

Now that we have explored the key elements of good storytelling, let's look at how we can use them in our speeches.

Some considerations when including stories in your presentation should be:

- What is your presentation's purpose?
- Should you include stories at all?
  - Where might stories be included?
  - What kind of stories might work?
  - Where can appropriate stories be found?
  - How should stories be told?

WHAT IS YOUR PRESENTATION'S MAIN PURPOSE?

When you have to present, consider the following to establish your objective.

Who Is Your Audience?

Your audience could be:

- A bunch of school kids;
- Dinner party guests;
- Managers at a corporate function.

Why Are They There?

Let's say that the:

- School kids are there to learn how to save money;
- Dinner party guests are present to celebrate a 21st birthday party;

- Managers have congregated to hear about some new technology for their people.

What Are They Expecting to Hear From You?

- The school kids are expecting to learn simple tips on how to save money;

- The dinner party guests are expecting you to honour the person whose 21st birthday they are celebrating;

- The managers are expecting insights as to the new technology and how it will help improve performance.

SHOULD YOU INCLUDE STORIES AT ALL?

This depends on your audience and their expectations. If you decide to include stories, ensure that they fit within the context of your presentation. Make your stories relevant to the experience and interests of your audience. For example, if you are speaking to a group of parents who have teenage children, tell a story that comes from your experience as a parent or as a teenager. Each story should have a point to it that your listeners can easily grasp and readily identify with.

WHERE MIGHT STORIES BE INCLUDED?

Stories are best introduced when you are making a point. If there are three points to your message, then you may want to include three separate stories or perhaps one story that covers all three points.

WHAT KIND OF STORIES MIGHT WORK?

Consider the following as a guide for including stories in your speech:

- Keep your stories short – two to three minutes at most. Leave out any unnecessary detail. Use your story to quickly clarify or support a point you're making, then move on.

- A good story puts information in perspective. It doesn't replace information.

- A good story paints a picture. It helps your listeners 'see' what you're saying.

- Make the characters in your story real so that your audience can identify with them.

- A good story is one you're comfortable telling and that is easy to recall (especially if you have experienced it first hand).

- And the most important point is this – personal stories (ones that are told from your own personal experience) are the best kinds of stories for four reasons:

  - Your audience will not have heard them in the public arena;

  - You have the elements of surprise and mystery on your side;

  - You can embellish the story if you wish;

  - Audiences love to hear stories told in the first person. So where possible, tell stories where you are part of the action.

WHERE CAN APPROPRIATE STORIES BE FOUND?

There are unlimited sources from which to find a good story. Stories can come from just about anywhere: from personal experience or the experiences of others, from books, newspapers and magazines, the Internet, movies and TV programs. Some speakers even use stories from mythology. You can also tell a story you've heard from someone else, just ensure that you credit the source.

HOW SHOULD STORIES BE TOLD?

When you are telling a story, put emotion into it. You are not reciting facts and informing as a newsreader would. You are telling a story and good body language (see Chapter 14) should support your anecdote. How you connect with your eyes, your gestures, posture, voice modulation and emotions should all be considered in an effort to enliven and add emotional power to your story. The effective use of these will help you connect with your audience in a powerful way.

Think of good speakers you've heard — perhaps a colleague, your CEO, a public figure, even a performer being interviewed. Listen for the ways in which they weave stories into their remarks.

Finally, make sure you practise your delivery. It may be best to practise in front of a trusted person who can give you honest feedback or even help to improve your story. Keep practising until you are ready to use stories to connect with your audience.

Summary

Here's what to do to connect to your audience with stories:

1. Elements of good storytelling are an attention-grabbing opening, establishing the situation, bringing emotion to the story, being creative and bringing it all together at the end.

3. Decide if you should include stories. Consider your audience and your allotted speech time. Ensure that your stories align to your message and have a point that your listeners can readily identify with.

4. Stories are best introduced when you are making a point. If your audience remembers the story, they will remember your point.

5. It's best to tell stories from your own personal experience; a good personal story, well told, will maximise impact.

6. Tell your stories with emotion; bring them

alive with your eyes, gestures, posture and voice modulation.

7. Finally, make sure you practise your delivery, best done with a trusted person who can provide feedback and help you improve the story. Practise until you are ready to tell the story that connects with your audience.

CHAPTER 11

Use Humour

*'If you don't have humour, then you may as
well nail the coffin lid down now.'*

Roger Moore

This chapter follows on from the storytelling chapter because there is a direct connection between the two. Often the best way to include humour is when you are telling a story.

I love the Australian sense of humour, especially the banter and gentle ribbing we give each other. It makes life so much more fun when you have people with a sense of humour around you; be it at work, play or home.

As a speaker, using appropriate humour will relax an audience and make them feel more comfortable listening to you. Humour can also help you to get your point across and break down barriers, thus making the audience more receptive to your ideas.

A Humorous Example

Here is an example of how I used humour to make a particular point. The story is in two parts and contains two separate incidents that eventually align together with a punchline.

My wife calls the first story 'Four go up, three come down.' It goes like this.

FOUR GO UP, THREE COME DOWN

My wife, Gayle, two teenage children and I were enjoying the many wonderful sights on a trip to Paris. We had had a particularly long day and it was raining when we found ourselves near the Arc de Triomphe. The kids and I quickly out-voted my wife that we should climb up the 284 steps to the very top. While the kids bounded up, I supported my wife up the winding stairway, suggesting that I could have kept pace with the kids if she had not slowed me down. Gayle ignored my ribbing, she always does.

When we finally reached the top, we enjoyed the fantastic views. After 20 minutes, with the light fading, the kids found me and decided they had seen enough, so we went to look for Mum. Well, we did a couple of circuits but could not find her in the dim light. One of the kids suggested perhaps she had gone back down and that we should descend the 284 steps to meet her. Here's where I made two mistakes.

Lesson one: Never heed the advice of a know-it-all teenager.

Lesson two: If you have a mobile phone, use it to locate your wife.

Did I mention how exhausted I was and therefore susceptible to making mistakes?

The kids and I carefully went down those steps and only towards the bottom entrance did I feel that all was not right. My worst fears were confirmed when there was no Gayle at the exit door, only the start of a ceremony for the eternal flame. We joined the other tourists to watch the ceremony as I wondered if Gayle was still at the top. Suddenly my mobile phone rang; it was Gayle with 'Where the hell are you?'

'Um. Down at the exit.' I replied sheepishly. What she said next is unrepeatable.

As she appeared at the exit and saw me, Gayle started to yell about how dare I leave her at the top. The people gathered for the eternal flame ceremony turned around to see what the commotion was. When Gayle saw that the ceremony was happening, she stopped in her tracks. We all slinked away slowly from the bewildered group pretending nothing had happened. On the way home I could feel my wife's fury, but now we can laugh (or at least I can) about 'four go up, three come down'.

FREE BOOZE

The second part of the story happened when we flew out of Europe. The plane had a 3-4-3 configuration, with Gayle and I seated together and the kids in front of us. The seat next to me was occupied by a young lady travelling on her own. This particular airline is generous with their service and that extends to serving alcohol. The young lady decided to avail herself of this generosity and started lining up three or four wine glasses on her tray.

The more she consumed, the more concerned I became about the effects of the alcohol, thinking that she would be sick all over me. She kept drinking and slurring when she attempted to speak with me. I thought this a dangerous sign of impending throwing up. So in an act of total self-preservation, I turned to Gayle and asked sweetly if she and I could swap places.

With a wry smile, she said, 'No, we can't. Remember the Arc de Triomphe'. That's all she needed to say! I knew there was nothing else I could do but accept my fate, seated between a vengeful woman and an intoxicated young lady.

Miracle of miracles! She did not throw up but ended up going to sleep peacefully … well peacefully for her at least, because her loud snoring kept me awake for the next few hours.

There ends the two episodes of how karma played out. I tell this story to make the point that you should always do the right thing. If I had done the right thing by Gayle at the Arc de Triomphe, perhaps she may have swapped seats with me on the plane. Karma bit me on the bottom and bit me hard. The moral of the story is to do good to others, and it will come back to you.

Self-Effacing Humour

A wonderful way to connect with an audience is through self-effacing humour. Self-effacing humour, or making fun of yourself, is where you find the humour of your own weaknesses. People who have the ability to laugh at themselves are more likely to be perceived as confident, strong and likeable.

With this type of humour, a little goes a long way, so the key is to not overdo it as it may appear that you have a negative outlook on life. Most people don't like people who take themselves too seriously, so have some fun picking on yourself.

One of the reasons self-effacing humour works is that people with low self-esteem and low confidence often feel the need to inflate themselves, while confident people don't need to remind others of how wonderful they are. Your listeners know that you are human and prone to failure, and they see that you are OK with sharing it. This type of humour is a very powerful magnet.

If can mock yourself, you are subconsciously sending a message to the audience that you feel confident and secure.

Most audiences can see right through speakers who are trying to big-note themselves. Nothing turns people off more than a show-off. Aussies love to cut down the show-off … it's called the tall poppy syndrome. An effective way to counter this is to let your audience have the upper hand in some way. Your audience would rather hear about the time you stuffed up, rather than the time you easily won the gold medal.

So what can you make fun of? Your physical appearance may be fair game, especially if you're a particularly tall, short, overweight or bald. Maybe you are a disorganised or forgetful person, you could tease yourself about that. If you can't read maps or have really bad table manners, you could use those examples. You may have a strange habit, such as waking up at midnight to eat salty caramelised macaroons, or an insecurity, such as checking that you have locked the front door ten times before you leave home. Use anything, as long as you are the target.

You don't have to limit the use of self-effacing humour to yourself personally. If you are a lawyer, you can make fun of the profession. Take all lawyers down with you (warning: they may sue). You may come from an ethnic background with its own cultural peculiarities. Make fun of those differences.

As a speaker, look for opportunities to poke fun at yourself. This will be one of your most powerful tools for connecting with the audience and a subtle way to show your self-confidence.

Adding Humour to Your Presentation

As a speaker, here are some things to remember when using humour in your speech.

MAKE SURE IT TICKLES YOUR FUNNY BONE FIRST!

If it's not funny to you, then you certainly cannot expect your audience to find it humorous. **Experiment with a small group.** Practising humour in front of one person may not provide an accurate reflection as senses of humour differ from person to person. However if you choose a small group, preferably of people who represent your larger audience, you can use them as your guinea pigs. Check out if this group enjoys your humour. Even if your experimental group does not laugh or smile initially, don't give up, because it may be in the way you are delivering the joke. Ask them what would make it better. It may take practice to get more comfortable in your delivery.

MEMORISE THE JOKE

Only use a joke in a speech after you are comfortable telling it from memory. Think of a time when someone had you going with a great story and then fluffed the punchline. It makes the story fizzle faster than a piping hot pizza shoved into a freezer. Make sure you practice the joke until you are ready to tell it to whoever is ready for a laugh.

START A HUMOROUS STORIES FOLDER

Start gathering stories that you find funny, even if they are only mildly amusing. These stories can be embroidered, made more colourful and given more depth with great word pictures. I use my smartphone to jot down stories and notes and these are instantly accessible to edit and use as the basis for new stories. A good practice is to create categories (in sub-folders) such as funny stories involving your children or humour you find in the workplace, so you can put your humorous anecdotes into these sub-folders. When you need a funny story for the right occasion, it will be easier and faster to pick it out from the right category.

ENSURE YOUR HUMOUR HAS A POINT

Unless your objective as a presenter is purely to entertain an audience (like a stand-up comedian), then your joke should always tie in with some aspect of your message.

For example, I tell the story of facing my fear when I came home one day and discovered the world's biggest huntsman boldly perched on the front door. I have a massive fear of spiders. But I thought 'This is an occasion to face my fear'. So, I courageously grabbed a broom, took aim and smashed the spider against the door. When it fell, I kept hitting it with the broom like a crazed madman … just to make sure it was really dead! I heard bursts of laughter from my wife and children as they opened the front door and told me, between hysterical fits of laughter, that the spider I had killed was a toy. I should have known, after all it was Halloween that day. The point I make with this story is that you can face your fear, have courage and kill the spider (or whatever fear you have), even if it is only a toy spider.

IDENTIFY HUMOUR IN YOUR EVERYDAY INTERACTIONS WITH OTHERS

Each day you probably encounter situations that put a smile on your face or make you laugh. It may be a person's weird reaction in response to something, quick-fire banter with a stranger or a funny story a work colleague shared. Put humour on your radar and you will start to see all types of everyday stories that you can use to connect with your audience.

Humour is simply another way of making a point to your audience, and it can help you be a more effective speaker. Remember, *'A smile is a curve that straightens out a lot of things.'*

Summary

1. Use humour to make a point. When preparing your presentation, look for opportunities to introduce a humorous anecdote, preferably a personal one.

2. Use self-effacing humour. Think about all the things you can make fun of yourself for. Are you really short and have to pack high shelves at the supermarket? Or a bus driver who is always getting routes mixed up? Be a human dartboard and throw darts at yourself. Your audience will love you for it.

3. Does the intended humour make *you* smile? Make sure you find it funny first, because if you don't then there's every chance your audience won't find it funny either.

4. Experiment with a small group. Always test your jokes out on friendly but honest

people. It's best to do it with diverse personalities to see if the joke resonates with all or most of them.

5. Memorise the joke. Ensure that you know it really well and have practised it. Humour is all about telling it exactly the way it should be told to get the right audience reaction.

6. Start a humorous anecdotes folder. Keep adding to this folder as you get more funny stories. Categorising your funny stories will make it easier to access the right one to make your point.

7. Your humour must have a point. Don't just tell jokes. You are not a stand-up comedian, you are a presenter. As a presenter you have a point or points to make. Make sure that your humour ties-in nicely with the point you are making.

8. Choose humour from everyday interactions. Put humour on your radar. Look for everyday funny situations that you can use to make your presentations more effective.

CHAPTER 12

Speak with Passion

'Passion is energy.
Feel the power that comes from
focusing on what excites you.'

<small>OPRAH WINFREY</small>

My wife and I celebrated my birthday by taking a three-day cruise around Sydney. It was advertised as a 'Food and Wine Experience' and we took full advantage of the opportunity to learn from the experts. What really impressed us was how passionate each speaker was about their product or service.

My wife and I had the good fortune of sharing a table for lunch with a famous vintner from the New South Wales Hunter Valley region who produces wines consumed all over the world. When the discussion turned to the topic of wine, there was an immediate sparkle in his eyes. He lived and breathed winemaking and the wine industry was his life. He evidently loved consuming wines from all over the world and not just the wines he produced. He was passionate about learning about excellent wines so that he could create these for his customers.

Another of the cruise's presenters was Kim McCosker, a young mother who had launched a famous brand of cookbooks with recipes using four ingredients or less. Her goal was to prepare meals quickly and easily to meet her family's expectations. McCosker realised that most mothers face a similar daily challenge. With this in mind she and her partner developed the concept of creating recipes that were quick, easy, healthy and cost effective. Many people have busy lives, and this type of cooking resonated with a lot of them. Thus was born the idea of cooking with four ingredients or less. Imagine! No more recipes with sixteen ingredients … only four! Kim's passion is to simplify cooking for the busy family.

What is Passion and How Do We Share It?

Passion is an intense emotion! Passion is a feeling of unbridled enthusiasm, strong desire and a magnetic attraction to something or someone.

When they have a passion for something people often want to do two things:

- Obtain as much knowledge as they can about it;

- Share their interest with others.

People are passionate about many things; they may have passion for a hobby, travel or simply living life.

I'm sure you are passionate about something. The question for speakers is how to share that particular passion with others.

So how can we speak passionately? In the rest of this chapter we are going to explore the following steps on how to develop and share your passion:

- Discover your passion;

- Become an expert;

- Develop a plan to share your passion;

- Execute the plan;

- Share your passion as a speaker.

DISCOVER YOUR PASSION

What is it that energises you when you first wake up in the morning, or what do you think about just before going to bed? Do you have a strong desire for travel and experiencing different cultures? Or helping orphans in a third-world country to have a better life? Perhaps you have a passion for creating beautiful bonsai gardens. Or your passion may be experiencing various teas from around the world. It could be anything.

Discovering one's passion may be easy for some and for others it may take a while. Enjoy the journey of discovery and where it leads you.

BECOME AN EXPERT

Once you know what your passion is, decide to become an expert on it. This will mean spending time to learn as much as possible about the topic. I have a friend whose passion is investing in quality shares and holding them for the long term.

He researches companies that come onto his radar with a fine-tooth comb before buying shares in them. On average he spends 20 hours a week researching, which is key to his success.

Only you can decide how much time you will devote to your passion. You may start with one hour per week and build it up. You may decide to choose a different passion. But once you decide, religiously allocate time each day to gain more knowledge about your subject. Use the Internet and talk to current experts to further your knowledge and, with time and focus, you will become an expert.

DEVELOP A PLAN TO SHARE YOUR PASSION

To prepare a plan for sharing your passion, ask yourself the following questions …

… about your audience:

- Are they novices seeking a basic understanding?
- Are they familiar with the topic but seeking further knowledge?

… about the channels will you use to convey your message:

- Will it be a stand-up presentation?
- Will it be via blogs or articles?

… about how you will connect with your audience:

- Will you involve your audience? And how?
- How will you make it unique so that your audience remembers you?

EXECUTE YOUR PLAN

The famous US tennis player Andre Agassi had a great work ethic. One of his mottos was 'plan your work, work your plan.' And he lived and breathed this in the meticulous manner he planned, prepared and executed his eight Grand Slam wins.

Agassi would consider the court surface, which racquets to use, and the weather (if a factor). He would also anticipate the game his opponent would play to try to exploit his weaknesses and he therefore ensured that an appropriate mitigation plan was in place.

Agassi would then take the plan and start to prepare through practice. Often he chose to practise with a player who had a similar style to his opponent; or get the practice player to play in that style. Then at game time Agassi would be well prepared to take on his opponent. And, in most cases, win!

Ensure you have a thorough plan, prepare well and finally execute (and win)!

How to Share Your Passion as a Speaker

USE POSITIVE ENERGY

The best way to share your passion with an audience is to use positive energy. Audiences will reflect that energy back. Demonstrate your love for your topic by having the right amount of positive energy. You don't have to go over the top, but do express that you are excited to be there and thrilled to share something special.

INVOLVE YOUR AUDIENCE

While it's great to speak about your passion, your audience will enjoy it more if they are intimately involved. You can invite them to ask questions, or play with a demo, or simply come up on stage and join in some fun game you've created to explain your passion.

TELL GREAT STORIES TO CONVEY YOUR PASSION

Telling stories is another way to get your audience to connect with your passion. Read Chapter 10, on telling stories, and add this element to your speech.

Summary

1. Discover your passion. Find out what you love to do. This may be something you instantly know or may discover through experimentation.

2. Become an expert. The more knowledge you have about your passion, the more you are able to share it with others. *Immerse* yourself in the topic to develop your expertise.

3. Share your passion. When seeking opportunities to share your passion,

consider your audience and how you will communicate and connect with them.

4. Prepare and execute your plan. Be well prepared to share your passion and deliver to exceed your audience's expectations.

5. Share your passion as a speaker. Use positive energy and body language. Simply smile and smile often. Involve your audience; get them to enjoy your passion as much as you do. Tell them great stories that connect with your passion.

CHAPTER 13

Show Vulnerability

'To share your weakness is to make yourself vulnerable; to make yourself vulnerable is to show your strength.'

<small>CRISS JAMI</small>

Can you show strength through demonstrating vulnerability? Most of us would think this is a paradox. We are judged on our success at work and in life by how confidently we behave. The stronger we look and behave, the more successful we are deemed to be. Yet to demonstrate real strength you need to reveal a chink in your armour, the vulnerability that makes you human.

Strength and vulnerability are not opposites. In fact, vulnerability requires high levels of strength and courage. It requires courage to be who we are despite our fears of not being accepted or liked. It requires that we unconditionally accept the parts of ourselves that we don't like or of which we are ashamed. It requires courage to talk about our failures and take responsibility for them. It requires courage to admit that we feel uncertain or that we don't know all the answers.

One great leader who demonstrated vulnerability was Nelson Mandela. During the memorial service for the legendary Mandela (also known as Madiba), US President Barack Obama spoke glowingly about Mandela as an icon, smiling and serene, detached from the tawdry affairs of lesser men. Obama stated how Madiba often shared with us his doubts and fears and his miscalculations along with his victories. The great Madiba openly shared his vulnerabilities.

How to Practise Vulnerability

Is it possible to show vulnerability? Yes it is, but it takes awareness, courage and practice. The following are some ways you can try.

BECOME SELF-AWARE

You can start simply by becoming more aware of when you feel vulnerable. Make a mental note or write down what makes you feel vulnerable. Is it when you are communicating with an executive at work? What about when you have a captive audience, are telling a joke and thinking 'Don't stuff up the punchline!'? Or when you are driving on the unfamiliar side of the road in a foreign country?

BE HONEST WITH YOURSELF

What are some qualities you believe that you need to hide from others? Perhaps you don't yet accept these things about yourself. Remember that what we don't accept about ourselves can derail us as some point, so becoming aware of your chinks is an important start to understanding what makes you vulnerable.

REVEAL YOUR CHINKS TO OTHERS

Practise revealing more about yourself to others. Perhaps start with people you implicitly trust, such as your spouse or sibling. As you become more confident (there's the paradox again), start to share your vulnerability with others. Look to share something about your background, your values, your story, or a failure you experienced and what you learned from it. For example, for many years I tried not to reveal to fellow Australians that I was born in Pakistan and grew up in what many consider a volatile country. I felt that revealing my birthplace would cast me in a negative light. So, I tried to 'Australianise' myself by downplaying the fact that I grew up in a third-world Muslim country.

This is despite the fact that I enjoyed growing up in Karachi. Only after I became more confident could I openly share about my early years living there as part of a Catholic minority. Now I am more than happy to share stories of growing up, of the good Muslim friends that I have, of the cultural wonders of that part of the world, and even of the war between India and Pakistan that scared the living daylights out of me at the age of nine.

Begin to reveal your chinks to others and see how it feels. Note their reaction; some may be positive and some may not (after all, we are all judgmental to varying degrees). When people are not positive, just take note of it and see how it makes you feel. You may feel the urge to hide that chink again. It will take courage to keep sharing your weakness.

STATE HOW YOU FEEL IN THE MOMENT

The next time you are feeling uncertain or embarrassed, openly state it. One way to do this is to preface it with 'I have a confession to make' or 'I'd like to share something'.

Most people can sense when you are uncertain, so opening up about it can show you as truthful and create an environment of greater authenticity and trust. When you show vulnerability, you subconsciously provide others with permission to share their own vulnerabilities and this can create honest conversations and strong bonds with others.

ADMIT WHEN YOU ARE WRONG

When you make a mistake, accept it and call it out. When you do this, especially if you are in a position of authority (as a parent, manager or mentor), it creates a space where others can also take accountability for failure, learn from it, and move on. Admitting when you are wrong shows that you have the courage to say that you are imperfect, and the compassion to accept yourself as you are (and thus accept others as they are), and the humility to say 'I am sorry.'

RECOGNISE WHEN OTHERS SHOW VULNERABILITY

When someone demonstrates vulnerability, congratulate them. Let them know that you admire their courage and honesty. They will be happy (and possibly surprised) to be recognised for 'coming out'.

CELEBRATE YOUR IMPERFECTIONS

Often we are our own worst critic. Each time we make a mistake or stuff up or show a weakness, we tend to beat ourselves up. Imagine if we changed our mindset instead to celebrate our stuff-ups with an inner 'high-five?' Consider making this change: rather than a beat-up, you forgive yourself and then congratulate yourself for being human.

How You Can Show Vulnerability As a Speaker

BE HUMAN

Being vulnerable as a speaker appears to be a paradox, especially when our mission as a speaker is to project confidence. However, demonstrating that you are vulnerable as a speaker provides your audience with an important perception. Vulnerability shows that you are simply being human.

Audiences do not like being preached at. And audiences do not warm to speakers who appear superior to them. Great speakers know this and they want their message to be heard and acted upon. The best way to achieve this is to show vulnerability. A chink in your armour. A chink that makes you human, one who has strengths but also faces challenges like any other human being.

As a speaker invariably there are opportunities for you to show vulnerability. One way to do this is to gain common ground with the audience. This could be through self-deprecating humour or sharing of a problem or issue that your listeners can relate to.

An example of a speaker who gained common ground with the Australian public is Anna Bligh. Bligh was Queensland Premier at the time of the 2010-11 floods in that state. The floods forced the evacuation of thousands of people with at least 90 towns and over 200,000 people affected. A visibly shaken Ms. Bligh fronted the media as she described the trail of devastation and hardship that now extended across the state to the capital, Brisbane. She was emotional as she addressed the nation: 'As we weep for what we have lost, and as we grieve for family and friends and we confront the challenge that is before us, I want us to remember who we are. We are Queenslanders. We're the people that they breed tough, north of the border.' Her emotional address touched the hearts, not just of Queenslanders but Australians across the nation.

SHARE SOMETHING OF YOURSELF

Depending on who your audience is, there is always something of yourself you can share. What problems do you and the audience have in common? Is there some personal challenge or weakness you have that you can share with them that makes you appear vulnerable?

As a speaker, firstly you need to accept yourself, warts and all. You need to love all of yourself. The more confident you are and the more you accept yourself, the more you can demonstrate your vulnerability when presenting.

Being vulnerable is about revealing more of you. Not bragging or bringing attention to yourself, but opening up about your fears, your doubts, your problems, your shortcomings.

LAUGH AT YOURSELF WHEN YOU MAKE MISTAKES

As speakers we want to give the perfect speech every time. While that is a good ambition to have, let's face it, none of us is perfect. We will make mistakes. Was there a time when you completely lost your train of thought when presenting or your mind went blank? Was that embarrassing for you? I remember going completely blank during a speech contest. For the life of me I could not remember my next line. I looked blankly at the audience, and they shifted uncomfortably and probably had sympathy for me. I eventually bumbled my way out of it, completed the speech and sat down feeling deeply embarrassed.

While I beat myself up at the time, I now look back on it as a learning experience. It will probably happen again, too. I need to be OK with it and able to make fun of myself in front of my audience. They are more likely to empathise with me and then hopefully I can pick up and re-connect with my audience. The listeners know that, like them, I'm human and we all make mistakes. Next time you make a mistake while presenting, make a short quip about it, laugh at your ineptitude, let the audience laugh with you and then move on.

ASK FOR YOUR AUDIENCE'S HELP

Often as a speaker, we are expected to be the expert on our topic. We are seen as the *go-to* person. But perhaps we don't know everything about the topic. Perhaps there is an aspect that we have been grappling with and there is no clear answer that comes. Is this an opportunity to show that you do not have all the answers? Absolutely!

Ask the audience for their ideas, feedback or solutions. Most people want to help. They will be more inclined to do this if they see a genuine need for help. Create that genuine need. Open your heart a little, show them that chink, ask for their help in fixing that chink. People will be more sympathetic towards you and happy that they are being given the opportunity to contribute to resolving your issue. What a great way to connect with your audience.

Summary

How to Practice Vulnerability

1. Become self-aware – make mental or written notes of when you feel vulnerable. Be honest with yourself when you assess your weaknesses.

2. Reveal your weaknesses to others - start with people you trust. Note how others react to your revelations.

3. Share how you feel in the moment – start with 'I have a confession to make …'

4. Admit when you are wrong – it takes courage and leadership to admit when you make mistakes. Admit it, call it out and move on.

5. Recognise and acknowledge when others

show vulnerability – let them know that you admire their courage and honesty.

6. Celebrate your imperfections – instead of beating yourself up for you inadequacies, accept them and give yourself an inner high-five.

How to be Vulnerable as a Speaker

1. Be human – audiences warm to speakers who show they are human and vulnerable. Share something of yourself - warts and all. Share your concerns, your problems with your audience. Be open, be honest.

2. Laugh when you make mistakes when you are presenting – let the audience laugh with you.

3. Ask for your audience's help – you are not perfect and do not know everything. Your audience will be sympathetic and want to help.

CHAPTER 14

Use Powerful Body Language

'I speak two languages, Body and English.'

MAE WEST

Body language can be defined as *non-verbal communication*, where thoughts, intentions, or feelings are expressed by physical behaviours, such as *facial expressions, body posture, gestures, eye movement, touch* and the *use* of space.

When you are presenting, powerful body language becomes an essential tool in helping you to build credibility, express your emotions, and connect with your audience. It also helps your audience to focus more intently on your message.

You may be unaware of the messages you are conveying non-verbally. When speakers see themselves on video, they're often surprised that their body language seems to convey an entirely different message than the one they had intended.

In my mid-twenties I participated in a public speaking training workshop.

As part of the workshop, each participant had to stand and deliver a short two-minute speech. Each speech was videoed and the facilitator used it to provide feedback. Watching my presentation was eye-opening for me. I didn't realise that I was jingling change in my pocket. How distracting for my audience!

Other participants demonstrated other body language distractions that they were not aware of because they were so focused on getting their message out. One participant kept rocking back and forth. An older gentleman had his hands behind his back throughout his presentation, while another shy-looking participant took the prayer stance. And then there was a young woman who kept constantly re-adjusting her skirt.

Watching and discussing these distractions was a great way to become aware of the type of body language that distracts. Awareness is the first step towards rectifying and replacing these distractions with good body language.

Now we will consider the types of body language that may be distracting to your audience or emit negative signals. After that we will review how to incorporate powerful body language to enhance your connection with your audience.

Negative Body Language

HANDS ON YOUR HIPS

When you stand with your hands on your hips, it may indicate that you are a 'know-it-all'. Your audience may perceive you to be arrogant or aggressive. Be conscious of where your hands are and keep them at your side and gesture naturally.

HANDS BEHIND YOUR BACK

As with hands on hips, this stance may be perceived as one of arrogance. As a speaker, the last thing you want is to be seen as arrogant, so never, ever present with your hands behind your back.

STEPPING BACK WHILE SEEKING A DECISION

When you step back or move away from your audience while asking for a decision, it expresses a lack of conviction and suggests you are fearful. Indeed you may be afraid that your audience will not accept your request, but if you step back, there is a possibility that you will encourage this response. The next time you ask for a decision from your audience, consciously take a step forward and ask with conviction. Your confidence will assure your audience and you'll maximise your chances of securing a positive response.

CROSSING YOUR ARMS
WHEN FACING QUESTIONS

In prehistoric times, people crossed their arms across their chest to protect their hearts when someone attacked them. Today, when communicating with others, crossing your arms across your chest is often seen as a defensive gesture (even though it may simply be a comfortable stance for you or perhaps you are feeling cold). When you use this gesture while facing questions from your audience, you look as if you are getting defensive or lacking confidence. It could also indicate that you are trying to hide something.

When presenting, always try to show your hands to demonstrate honesty and transparency and this will help build credibility with your audience.

POINTING FINGERS AT THE AUDIENCE

I worked with a project manager who had a habit of finger pointing during meetings. People felt intimidated by him and he often received negative reactions because of this. Whether he did this intentionally as a power play or unconsciously, it did him no favours in building trust with work colleagues.

Be conscious of the way you use your fingers when communicating with others. Eliminate the need to point at others. After all, most of us are peace-loving creatures. Any act of aggression can unsettle us and make us feel threatened.

If you do need to point, then do it away from your audience. This was very effectively done during a speech contest I attended where the presenter was describing how someone pointed a gun – he pointed his finger (representing the gun) away from the audience (towards the exit door). The audience got the point and did not feel threatened in any way.

BEGGING STANCE

Have you observed speakers who hold up their palms when speaking as if seeking alms? It looks like they are either begging to be heard or seeking favours or simply that they seem nervous. This also may be a speaker's way of trying to convey humility, but it does not resonate well with most audiences. The begging stance is often seen as weakness or nervousness, so be conscious of this.

PACING RESTLESSLY

Some presenters have a habit of pacing up and down as they speak. When you pace the room, your audience may find it difficult to concentrate on your message as they are more focused on your movements. Using the breadth of your speaking platform to enhance your message is greatly encouraged, as long as you are not distracting your audience. If you are moving around, gauge your audience's response and see if they are being distracted. If it appears that they are, then just stop and centre yourself to get them focused back to your main message.

Body Language that Connects

Effective body language supports your message and projects a strong image of you as a presenter. Audiences respond best to presenters who appear lively and energetic. Audiences appreciate movement when it is meaningful and supportive of the message. Presenters who care deeply about their message will tend to use their entire bodies to support the message.

During a Public Speaking International Convention I watched a speaker present about his journey to the summit of Everest. He was the first of his countrymen to reach the summit. He spoke in front of an audience of 2000 people and his presentation went for 45 minutes.

During the whole presentation, he stood fixed in the middle of a very large speaker's platform, using very few gestures and movements. He had a great story to tell and yet I felt something was missing. To me it was a shame that he did not use his body language to mirror the compelling story, as this would have had a more dramatic impact on his captive audience.

Motivational speaker Nido Quebein said on the subject of gestures 'I think a speaker loses much when he or she stands there without any gestures, without any emotions, and delivers the presentation – versus the speaker who emotionally gets involved in what he or she is saying. I believe that gestures should definitely be used because God did not create us to be a rock. I want people to look at me and say "He's feeling what he's doing".'

Anyone can utter a series of words; it is the presenter's personal connection to those words that can bring them to life for the audience. Think of a presenter you have observed whose gestures were magnified as if to embrace the whole room. Recall a speaker who came up close to the audience in an attempt to really connect with them. How about the speaker whose face expressed their passion while their eyes connected as if speaking to each member of the audience.

GESTURES

When you think gestures, you think hands. As a presenter they do not belong in your pockets jingling change. They should not be folded across your chest or behind your back. Your hands are your tools to naturally convey your message, emphasise a point, express emotion, release tension, and ultimately engage your audience.

Most people already have gestures at their disposal. I remember one manager who used the same gestures repeatedly. She would place one hand with the palm facing upwards and the other hand over it moving in a clockwise direction. That was her gesture to use when explaining concepts.

Think about your own gestures. For example when you wave hello at someone, do you do a little wave with your hand around mid-chest? Do you wave with your fingers? Do you wave with an almighty flourish? Or perhaps it's something in between, depending on the situation.

Think of a gesture that supports words such as 'large' or 'tiny'. The gestures to support 'large' could be extending both hands apart as much as you can, while 'tiny' can be gestured using two fingers with a minute space between them.

Gestures you use in everyday conversation tend to be smaller than ones you would use in front of an audience. When you are presenting, you need to scale your gestures to the size of the room and the size of the audience (think depth and breadth). The most effective gestures arise from the shoulder, not the wrist or elbow. Shoulder gestures have more impact as they create the illusion that the presenter is occupying more space and this should complement your energy as you present your message.

Stance

Stand When Presenting

Standing to make a presentation is, in most cases, more persuasive than sitting. This particularly applies when you have an audience of 10 or more. If less than that, it may be best to sit and present as you will connect better with a smaller audience if you are part of the group.

For the larger audience, when you stand you show that you are the centre of attention. Along with the heightened physicality of your gestures, the volume of your voice should also increase. This will create a more cohesive delivery that greatly enhances your command and the impact of your message.

Display Confidence from the Get-Go

Your audience is judging you even before you have uttered a single word. You should walk up to the speaking area as a positive, confident person. Take your time and centre yourself before you commence speaking. Your stance will indicate in a matter of seconds whether you're happy, scared, confident, or uncomfortable. Audiences can read your body language. *Stance speaks.* A balanced stance with weight even but slightly forward tends to say that the speaker is engaged with the audience. A slumped stance can say that you are not confident or are unhappy to be there.

Hands and Feet

Your feet should point straight ahead, and you should appear natural. When you are not using your hands to gesture, place your hands gently by your side. Leaving your hands by your side between gestures can project that you are calm and this will reflect that you are in control. Another benefit is that these moments of stillness will enhance the effect when you do amplify your gestures. Be animated with your gestures when warranted and punctuate that movement with stillness.

Maximise Use of the Speaking Platform

Use the speaking platform to maximise impact. Staying in the one spot is not a good option. Always elect to have a lapel mike if possible so that you can utilise the platform rather than being stuck behind a lectern. The platform is your domain and you should use the breadth and depth of it to enhance your message.

I have seen good presenters using the breadth of the platform when they are speaking about a timeline. When most speakers gesture about the past and future, they use their right hand to indicate the past (the audience's left) and their left hand to indicate the future (the audience's right). This makes sense to the audience as you are presenting them with a linear progression of time from their left to their right.

Use the depth of the platform to truly connect with audience. For personal messages or particular points that you really want to resonate, come close to the edge of the platform. When you are using magnified gestures, use the back end of the platform so that the audience does not feel threatened by your amplified gestures.

FACIAL EXPRESSIONS

Use of facial expressions, including the movement of your eyes, mouth, and facial muscles, can either undermine your message or help you to connect with your audience.

Eye Contact

Making eye contact with your audience is essential if you want to be seen as a credible and confident presenter. Always ensure that you are making eye contact with someone in your audience. An effective method is to speak to one person (or for larger audiences, speak to a section) for one sentence or a few seconds, locking in eye contact with them. Then move onto the next person or section.

Ensure that you cover all of the audience at some stage during the presentation. This way no-one will feel left out. If possible, ensure that you make eye contact evenly. Some speakers tend to only focus on the right side or the left side or right up the middle. By doing this they are alienating some of their audience, no matter how effective their message.

Expressing Emotions

Eyes are critical in forming our facial expressions. It is said that 'eyes are the windows to the soul'. Eyes provide a great insight to what emotions you are experiencing at the time. Wide eyes may demonstrate great fear or surprise. Narrowing of eyes might convey distrust of others or defensiveness.

Here are some emotions that you can demonstrate with facial expressions.

Sadness

It's the look in your eyes that telegraphs the sadness you're feeling. Feel the emotion and let your eyes do what comes naturally. Even if your eyes look down to convey sadness, try and still look at your audience when possible, so as not to break the connection you have already created with them.

You can display sadness with tears in your eyes. If you are speaking about a sad personal situation, tears may well up within you. Your mouth can be used in a downward 'u' shape to demonstrate sadness. A furrowed brow, wringing hands and slumped shoulders are all indicators of feeling sad.

Your connection with your audience must be authentic. Take your time to convey sadness … your audience should feel your pain and at the very least feel sympathetic. Nothing can disengage an audience from a speaker faster than if they sense the emotions are merely an act.

I have seen some speakers convey sadness when talking about the death of a loved one or loss of something. Use this powerful experience if it is appropriate and, in that moment, you will have a real connection with people.

Irritation or Exasperation

One of my children's favourite pastimes is to roll their eyes each time I make a statement that they do not agree with or they think is absurd or embarrassing. As a dad, I feel it's my job to get as many of these eye-rolls as possible because I know that I have hit their annoyance buttons.

As a speaker, you can easily show exasperation by rolling your eyes towards the sky. An eye-roll does need to accompany what you are saying; either when you are expressing annoyance or feeling exasperated about something. The eye-roll can be subtle and this may be the best way to convey the emotion to your audience.

Your body can also be used effectively to convey exasperation. Think how you would do it naturally when someone or a situation really gets to you. Perhaps a demonstrable throw of the hands in the air as if to say 'I just give up', or a deep sigh along with a shake of your head as if to convey 'I don't believe this'. A strong exhalation of breath, clenched fists, hands being raked through one's hair, rubbing the back of the neck, or even dragging the hands over cheeks, chin or jaw are all other ways we can express frustration in real life. Try experimenting with some of these.

The combination of your voice, body and facial expressions can be used effectively to convey how irritated or exasperated you feel about someone or something.

Suspicion

Suspicion is another emotion you can express with your eyes. You can do this by narrowing your eyes and looking sideways. Or cocking your head and turning the body away slightly. This could show that you are skeptical of what is being said or done, or just plain suspicious. Perhaps you can use this as an adjunct to humour; being skeptical of a competitor's farcical claims about their product or service. Think about using it when you are conveying a dialogue with a person who is cheating or doing the wrong thing.

Another way to demonstrate skepticism is to arch your brow as if to say 'Really? I don't believe a word you are saying'.

Love

There are many ways to express one of the strongest emotions: love.

Using your eyes to display love is a natural thing. When you are talking about love, be it for your life-long partner, your beautiful child or your nurturing parent, the emotion of love may automatically be displayed in your eyes. When you are talking about love, feel it in your body and it will be seen in your eyes.

Your face should have a soft smile when you are speaking about love. Your body should be relaxed. Use your hands to gesture in a non-aggressive manner. Love can be soft and gentle and should be conveyed that way.

Anger

Anger is a really versatile emotion for expression. It can be a *flash* in your eyes along with *flaring nostrils*. As with the emotion of love, feel the anger building within you and your eyes will attest to your feelings.

A passionate presenter uses their whole body to express anger. They can use their voice in a calm, quiet, intense but controlled manner or they can speak in a loud, aggressive tone. Their body language will match their voice with either controlled aggression or in-your-face guestures. The eyes can be aligned too – cold sniper eyes to display controlled anger, or blazing eyes for openly hostile anger.

Watch how politicians use body language when they are angry about their opponent's policies and ideas (which is often). Consider their body language, voice and the look in their eyes.

Politicians are practised actors and you can learn a lot from observing how they behave.

Most importantly, ensure that the audience members are not feeling threatened by your actions, rather that they feel the emotion of anger along with you.

Joy

Joy is a wonderful emotion to convey. There is something within your eyes, within you, that can reveal your joy to the whole world. You can show this in the way that your eyes light up, with surprise, love or happiness.

As when demonstrating the emotion of love, your body should convey a happy demeanour and a wonderful open energy. The main difference between conveying the emotions of love and joy is that joy should be very expressive and have great energy. While love can be conveyed with gentle body movements, joy should be *celebrated* with your body. Throw your arms in the air, smile wholeheartedly, radiate your inner energy; the chest is open, the shoulders are back, the chin is raised and all these actions will convey the bliss and ecstasy that you are feeling about the situation. Do this, and hopefully your audience will feel elated too!

Summary

Avoid Negative Body Language

1. Hands on your hips – this can be viewed as aggression or arrogance. Avoid this stance if you want to connect with your audience.

2. Hands behind your back – this stance can also be perceived as arrogance.

3. Stepping back while seeking a decision – this may appear as an expression of fear. If you want a decision from your audience, consciously take a step forward and ask with conviction.

4. Crossing your arms when facing questions – this is often seen as a defensive gesture or suggests a lack of confidence when facing your audience. Always position your hands openly to demonstrate honesty and transparency.

5. Pointing fingers at your audience – this is often seen as an aggressive behaviour. Be conscious of the way you use your fingers when communicating with others.

6. Begging stance – this is viewed as requesting or seeking favours. Be conscious of not using this stance when speaking.

7. Pacing restlessly when presenting – this can be distracting for your audience. Be conscious of how you use the speaker's platform and ensure your movements are enhancing your message and not detracting from it.

Body Language that Connects

Use gestures to enhance and not detract from your message. Use your hands to convey your message, emphasise a point, express emotion, release tension, and engage your audience:

1. Consider your stance to maximise impact.

2. Stand when presenting, unless to a group of less than 10.

3. Walk confidently to the platform, centre yourself, have a balanced stance.

4. Be animated with your gestures and punctuate those movements with stillness.

5. Use the breadth and depth of the speaking platform's to enhance your message.

Use facial expressions to convey emotions:
1. Sadness – use teary eyes, dismayed mouth and body to telegraph the sadness you're feeling.

2. Exasperation or irritation – use the eye-roll or throw up your hands to convey this feeling.

3. Suspicion – narrow your eyes or cock your head and turn your body slightly away to display suspicion.

4. Love – a soft smile, radiant face and gentle, relaxed movements should convey love.

5. Anger – demonstrate anger by a flash in your eyes, flaring nostrils, or aggressive movements.

6. Joy – displaying lots of positive energy, use your whole body to express celebration.

CHAPTER 15

Cultivate Charisma

'The reason we're successful, darling?
My overall charisma, of course.'

FREDDIE MERCURY

Entertainer Ricky Martin oozes it! Actress Julia Roberts emanates it! Former Australian Prime Minister Bob Hawke definitely has it! What is it that they share in common? It's that wonderful, alluring thing called charisma.

The word charisma comes from the Greek word for 'gift' – implying that certain people are bestowed at birth with the ability to be magnetic to others.

So, what exactly is charisma? During a workshop about presentation skills, I asked participants this question and no-one could quite provide a definitive description. One described it as being an extrovert, another said that it was being bold or courageous and yet another remarked that a charismatic person was simply a smooth talker.

While most people may not be able to articulate the definition of charisma, people seem to recognise when they see a *charismatic* person. They can point to famous people, leaders of nations, CEOs, actors, etc and identity that they have charisma, that certain *je ne sais quoi*.

Having charisma is vital to connecting with your audience, and here is the good news … charisma *can* be cultivated.

The Charisma Quotient

In the 1980s Ronald E. Riggio authored *The Charisma Quotient*, in which he described six traits displayed by charismatic people.

They are:

1. EMOTIONAL EXPRESSIVENESS

Charismatic individuals express their feelings spontaneously and genuinely. This allows them to influence the moods and emotions of others. Charismatic people may light up the room when they enter. They have an immediate impact (mostly positive) on the mood of the room.

2. EMOTIONAL SENSITIVITY

This is the ability to read others' emotions, and it allows the charismatic person to make an emotional connection by responding to their feelings. In Chapter 16, Care for Your Audience, you can read about the Australian diplomat who made each person feel as if they were the only person in the universe that he was connecting with at that time.

3. EMOTIONAL CONTROL

Truly charismatic individuals have the ability to control and regulate their emotional displays. They are good emotional actors, who can turn on the charm when they need to.

4. SOCIAL EXPRESSIVENESS

This is a verbal communication skill, demonstrated by the ability to engage others in social interaction. Charismatic people are skilled and entertaining conversationalists.

5. SOCIAL SENSITIVITY

This is a skill in reading and interpreting social situations, being able to listen to others, and be 'in tune' with them. Charismatic people are sensitive to their surroundings and diplomatic as the situation demands.

6. SOCIAL CONTROL

Charismatic people play a sophisticated social role every day. This allows them to fit in with all types of people and make emotional and social connections that distinguish them. One example of this is former Australian governor general Quentin Bryce. She carries herself with grace and poise – a certain physical presence that connects with others. She exhibits the same kind of authoritative calmness as Burmese politician Aung San Suu Kyi.

The Journey to Becoming a Charismatic Presenter

There are ways to become more charismatic. If this is a focus for you, then you can consider the following suggestions.

MAKE IT YOUR MISSION TO BRING JOY

Let me introduce you to a character I refer to as the *'Santa Claus Bus Driver'*. This anecdote will illustrate how you can change your behaviour and do this one simple thing to become more charismatic.

On a chilly winter's morning, I caught the bus into the city. Greeting me with a wonderful burst of energy and cheerfulness was the bus driver, with a 'Good morning, and how are you today?' What a delightful start to my day. I was not the only one who received warm salutations from this bus driver. Each passenger that got on the bus received a 'Top of the morning, sir' or 'Have a great day'. He even had some witty comments to make to some of his regular customers. All of this said with a genuine smile and sincerity.

I loved the way this bus driver interacted with the passengers. With each greeting, it was as if he brought a little joy into each person's life – a little gift like Santa Claus brings to kids at Christmas.

It boosted my mood that dreary day and I felt good for the rest of the day. Imagine if all of us consciously and genuinely brought a little joy to everyone we interacted with? I commit to doing my bit, how about you?

If you want to develop charisma, you can start by *bringing a little joy to other people*.

Most people will return the favour by smiling back at you, and perhaps greeting you in the same energetic way. Charismatic people bring joy to others. People can't wait to see or meet a charismatic person because that person, in some way, makes them *feel happier*. So, choose to develop more charisma by giving a little joy at each interaction you have with others.

As a speaker, it is vital that you bring some of that 'joy' to others. This may be by injecting your own brand of humour or sharing personal anecdotes. It may by inspiring or motivating them towards a better life. Or it may even be in the form of hope. If you can provide hope to your audience, then they may be able to see sunshine penetrating through even the dark clouds on a dreary winter's day.

USE YOUR NATURAL CHARISMA

Charismatic speakers are self-confident and assured. They exude buoyancy and ease when presenting.

So, if self-confidence is a requirement for charisma, think about situations in your life when you feel secure and confident. Perhaps it's when you are with your children as you tell them wonderful bedtime stories. Perhaps you are most relaxed and confident when you are with your spouse around the dinner table or with friends enjoying the banter. Think about the flow of the conversation during these occasions. How stress-free is it to speak with these people? Perhaps the conversation is easy and the words come out perfectly. The people you are connecting with are laughing. They are very interested in what you are saying. These are perfect situations to take note of, when you are just being your natural self and naturally charismatic.

Go on a discovery mission and contemplate when you are at your most confident with others. Ask yourself under what circumstances does this occur, who are you with, where and when. We all demonstrate charisma in certain situations. The challenge is to translate the same charisma that you have in those special situations to when you are presenting to an audience.

DISCOVER YOUR SPECIAL CHARISMA

Becoming a charismatic presenter is about:

- Being relaxed;

- 'Owning' the situation;

- Allowing your unique personality to show.

So what does charisma mean to you? Is it having a dazzling smile, a confident exterior, or that certain swagger? Define what charisma means to you and cultivate it.

The following is a further list of traits that charismatic people commonly have. You probably have some, if not all of them.

- Passion (for a topic, for people, a particular cause);

- Humour (use your special brand of humour, enjoy yourself, be playful, happy);

- A smile (this is the one universal language, use it);

- Knowledge (special knowledge of a particular topic);

- Positivity (everyone can become more positive with a change of attitude);

- Body language (bigger gestures, facial movements and stance can change perceptions);

- Inspiration (through trail blazing, or standing up for rights, or simply caring for a cause).

The next step is to self-analyse how much you have for each characteristic. Do you have a great smile that you use often? Keep using this trait.

Perhaps you assess yourself as being low on energy when speaking with others. If so, then this may be an area you need to focus on to become more charismatic.

All of the above characteristics are covered within this book in various chapters. After your self-assessment, determine which of these characteristics you want to focus on to develop more charisma and let your journey begin.

EMBEDDING CHARISMA INTO PRESENTATIONS

Once you've identified the characteristics of your unique charisma, it's time to bring that charisma into your presentations. Focus on a few characteristics that you want to improve on and obtain feedback from trusted friends to see if you are improving.

Charismatic speakers are not afraid to develop a unique style that their audience can recognise and come to expect from them.

Will you be the presenter who:

- is always genuine and true to one specific message?

- has props with every presentation?

- has wonderful, infectious energy?

- always involves his audience?

If you choose some of these to be your unique charismatic characteristics, then make them your trademark so that your audience can regularly expect them of you.

BECOME BIGGER

Another way to develop charisma when presenting is to become 'bigger': embellish your natural charisma so that it's almost larger than life. Always remember to be authentic otherwise the audience will see it as acting or going over the top and you may not connect with them as intended. So, when you are presenting remember to turn up the volume a little. It's still you, but a larger-than-life version.

Be conscious of audience size. For smaller audience groups, turn up the volume a notch, for larger audiences feel free to become more animated. Check how your audience is reacting. If they are recoiling in their seats (and this is not what you want in an audience response), pull back a little. If they seem to be lapping it up, keep at this level. If they are falling asleep, give yourself a swift kick (use your imagination) and turn it up a notch or two.

The more you can become bigger than your normal self, the greater chance that your audience will remember you and your *message*.

DEVELOP PRESENCE

You can demonstrate presence right from the very start of your presentation. When it is your turn to present, take control. You are in charge. Your audience is captive; they are bound to listen to what you have to say. This does not mean that you can take advantage of them, just that you can take advantage of the situation when you come up to the speaking platform.

Even before you speak, remain calm as you look over and smile at your audience. This will give you time to collect yourself before you launch. This also gives the audience the time to 'size' you up.

When they see that you are in total control they will consider that you have *presence*. Of course, you have to back this up with the right messages to 'earn' that presence.

PHYSICAL APPEARANCE

Charismatic speakers look good, they have stage presence. Looking good can mean an appealling physical appearance. Or it may mean how a person carries themselves, how they speak, how they dress and how confidently they present themselves.

As a presenter who wants to become more charismatic, your physical appearance is an important consideration to bear in mind if you want to have an instant rapport with your audience.

If you do not consider yourself particularly attractive then there are ways to increase the odds in your favour. Start paying greater attention to what you wear, your personal grooming and that all-important smile.

Research into charismatic presenters has found that speakers who shift posture more often, use more smiles, gestures and eyebrow-raises appear more charismatic.

Use these clues to becoming more attractive in everyday interaction with others and it will start to become second nature when you get up and speak.

Summary

Very few of us are born with charisma. Here is a summary of what you can do to develop it.

Become aware of Riggio's six traits:

1. Emotional expressiveness – do you light up the room with your mood?

2. Emotional sensitivity – do you make other people feel special?

3. Emotional control – can you turn on the charm when the occasion arises?

4. Social expressiveness – do you hold court at the pub or dinner party?

5. Social sensitivity – are you diplomatic when the situation requires it?

6. Social control – do you carry yourself with the appropriate grace and poise?

Bring joy – make it your mission to bring joy to your audience. Start by trying to bring a little joy to someone every day.

Use your natural charisma – self-assess the times when you are at your most confident with others. Apply this learning to further develop your charisma.

Discover your special charisma – focus on specific areas that will help you strengthen your charisma.

Embed charisma into presentations – define your unique presenting style and ensure that you embed it into all your speeches so that your audience identifies your unique style.

Become bigger – embellish your natural charisma to become larger than life (while still retaining your authenticity).

Develop presence – use the platform to take control right from the start. Remain calm, let your audience size you up. Back it up with a great message.

Physical appearance – looks matter. Use your looks to your advantage, dress to impress, use your dazzling smile and pay attention to how you carry yourself.

CHAPTER 16

Care for Your Audience

*'Nobody cares how much you know,
until they know how much you care.'*

THEODORE ROOSEVELT

Care is fundamentally important for speakers. This chapter tackles the topic in depth and has been divided into two sections:

- Respect your audience;
- Have compassion.

Respect Your Audience

The number one rule of all great speakers is to respect your audience. You will only get the audience's respect if you respect them first. You need to respect your audience:

- Before the speech;
- During the speech;
- After the speech.

BEFORE THE SPEECH

Every speaker has an obligation to know what their listeners are expecting from them. Are they expecting an entertaining speech? Are they expecting to hear how to deal with their teenage children?

In my early days as a speaker, I thought I would connect with the audience by using sporting analogies. On one particular occasion, I packed my speech with horse-racing jargon. The problem was that I did not bother to find out who my listeners were or what they expected to hear. When I arrived at the presentation, a significant percentage of the audience were businesswomen, who, I later found out, did not particularly care about horse racing.

After the speech the event coordinator tactfully informed me that non-sporting analogies may have received a better reception from that audience. I have never forgotten that experience … always respect your audience. Respecting your listeners before the speech is about understanding who they are and what they want.

What Are Your Audience's Beliefs?

To understand who your listeners are, determine their beliefs. For example, do they believe in equality for women in the workplace? Your speech should directly or indirectly align to what your audience's belief is.

What Are Their Demographics?

Determine the demographic of your audience. For example, are they mainly twenty-year-old women from a university-educated background?

Ensure that your message caters for this demographic group or modify it to bond better with this audience.

What Are They Expecting to Hear?

Determine what your audience is expecting to hear and how it fulfils their particular need. Will you solve a problem, entertain them with your wit, or influence them to volunteer for something?

Why Do They Want to Hear It From Me?

Establish why you are the source that will help them. For example, what is your expertise to help your audience of accountants understand the new laws imposed on their industry?

By thoroughly researching your audience before the presentation, you are respecting their needs and you will be in a much stronger position to meet their expectations.

DURING THE SPEECH

Respect for your audience during the speech is paramount to your integrity as a speaker. This means being constantly alert for audience reactions to your message.

Be on the Alert For Non-Verbal Clues

As a speaker you will be judged from the moment you walk on stage. You may find in the early stage of your presentation that some male audience members have their arms folded across their chest. This can be construed as 'Dear presenter, prove to me that you are worthwhile listening to'. Good presenters will win over their audience with a strong message that builds credibility.

As a presenter, there is nothing more deflating than becoming aware of clues from the audience that are less than flattering. Take the time when I was in a speech contest and halfway through my speech noticed an elderly gentleman starting to nod off. This sounded *warning bells* for me. Sleepy nods soon turned to soft snores. The warning bells turned into alarm bells as it slowly dawned on me that this was not just any audience member. The offending snorer happened to be the chief judge at the contest. How embarrassing! I took heart later on when other contestants confirmed that they received the same drowsy response from the tired judge.

So, what do you do when you encounter an audience (or for that matter, one or two key audience members) not responding the way you expected? You could vary or pick up the pace of your talk, speak a little louder than normal, get them involved in an activity, or select audience members to answer your questions (this technique is sure to wake up any audience, as each member begins to dread being the chosen one).

What About Verbal Clues?

If your speech includes question and answer time, the audience will expect an opportunity to ask questions or offer an opinion. This is another crucial point at which to respect your audience. In fact this is probably the most crucial time as this is where you leave a lasting impression.

A Chairman's Snub

A few years ago at a breakfast meeting I attended, the keynote speaker was the chairman of a major bank addressing about 100 bank employees. Following his presentation, one young man posed a question to the chairman. The young man asking the question was not particularly articulate and struggled to frame his question clearly. Rather than seek to understand the question, the chairman dismissed the enquiry with these exact words: 'Sorry, but your question is not grabbing me.' And then, oddly enough, the chairman turned to the audience and said 'Next question.'

Imagine the embarrassment the young man would have felt at this snub. A few minutes later, while the question and answer session was still in progress, the young man stood up and walked out of the presentation in full view of everyone. I felt for this young man. He did not deserve the response he got from the speaker. Perhaps by walking out, he was showing that the chairman's presentation had not grabbed him.

As speakers it is our *moral obligation* to respect all of our audience.

Respecting our audience means keeping their self-esteem intact no matter how they respond to our message or what questions they ask us. It means giving them truthful answers to questions they ask us, not spinning our answers as a politician might.

In summary, respect your audience throughout your presentation, paying particular attention to their non-verbal and verbal signs and messages … and rest assured, they will respect you in return.

AFTER THE SPEECH

If you want to leave a lasting impression, after the speech is the perfect time to give respect to your audience. You will obtain an audience's respect if you make yourself available after the formal presentations. This may be directly after your speech, or after all formalities have ended.

Respect from an Australian Diplomat

A few years ago, I attended a business seminar conducted by Austrade to promote business in the United Arab Emirates (UAE). The main speaker was a high-ranking Australian diplomat to the region. I was captivated by his deep knowledge of the UAE, the business culture there and the numerous opportunities for Australian businesses. But what really impressed me was the way he interacted with his audience after his presentation.

During the tea break, the MC invited the audience to line up for an opportunity to speak with the diplomat. With the smell of freshly brewed coffee and warm muffins tantalising my nostrils, I joined a long line of people queuing up to talk to him. What impressed me was that each time the diplomat spoke with a person, it was like there was no-one else in the universe that mattered to him except the person in front of him. That person had the diplomat's full and undivided attention. The diplomat listened intently to what that person had to say and then engaged them in conversation until they had completed their discussion. He then thanked them, warmly shook their hand and then moved on to the next person, with renewed attention.

When it was my turn, I made the observation to him that I thought he demonstrated great respect and care for his audience. He smiled and said 'How can they respect me, if I don't respect them first?' That is a fantastic attitude to have. Respect your audience first and they will, in turn, respect you. Care for them first, and they will care for you.

I'm sure that many people in that long queue will remember their interaction with that diplomat. Even after many years, I certainly do.

Meeting with your audience shows that you are interested

in them in a less formal setting. Some may have questions or comments about your presentation. I call this time 'audience listening time', because it's when I get to hear what the audience has to say. Your audience will respect you for your politeness and consideration and may relish the encounter with you. An important benefit for you is that they may provide valuable feedback on what messages resonated with them and, just as importantly, what did not. This will aid you in improving your message for future.

Have Compassion

Rules are meant to be broken, right? Society is governed by laws. Our daily lives are governed by rules and regulations. Students are governed by school rules. Motorists have to obey traffic rules. Employees must adhere to company policies. Rules are often in place to ensure order and compliance. But there are times when the rules may need to be changed or an exemption provided to do the right thing.

LAURA'S YEAR 10 FORMAL

Laura was a Year 10 student at a well-known girls school in Sydney. Like any other sixteen-year-old, she was excited about the upcoming school Formal. It was an opportunity to get dressed up in formal evening wear, look beautiful and attend the function with her friends. To get ready to look her best for the big day, she joined her mum at the gym. For two whole months, she went to the gym on a daily basis. She plucked up the courage to ask a boy to the Formal, and was delighted when he accepted.

As soon as her exams were over she focused more than ever on trying to perfect the evening. She even confessed to her mother that she saw this event as the second-most important day in her life (her future wedding day being the most important). Her father, someone close to me, felt immensely proud of Laura's dedication and commitment. He was sure that she was going to have a truly memorable evening at the Formal.

Then something happened that changed everything.

Two days before the Formal, Laura missed her school bus. She made a grave decision to wag school and go instead to the local shopping centre. Her parents were only made aware of the situation when the school contacted them because of her absence. Her parents were furious with her.

Because this was the second time that Laura had wagged school during the year, the school decided to take a strong stance. The day before the formal, they informed Laura that she would not be able to attend the Formal as pun ishment.

As you can imagine, Laura was devastated. This important event that she was so looking forward to was ruined by her decision to wag school. Laura's mother phoned the school to see if there was an alternative punishment. Given Laura's past record, the school believed that the punishment was appropriate and would stand.

Laura made the embarrassing phone call to her Formal partner to inform him of what had happened and that they would not be attending the formal. She was not the only one who was upset.

Laura's parents too felt many emotions that evening. They were angry with Laura for spoiling this opportunity by making a dumb decision. They felt disappointed with the school for making what they considered a harsh decision. They had spent many hours supporting Laura for this event and felt upset for her.

That night Laura's father spent a sleepless night. He needed to make a decision whether he should contact the school in the morning to see if they would change their minds or whether he should accept the decision. If he were to contact the school, what could he say to influence them to reverse the decision? By the early hours of the morning, he had made up his mind.

Laura's father had decided to contact the school … in person. He decided that he would discuss the matter with the Principal with a view to working out an alternative punishment.

The Principal was kind enough to meet him impromptu. The discussion commenced with the Principal providing an objective view of the circumstances followed by the reasons for the decision not to allow Laura to attend the Formal. Laura's father agreed that a penalty was in order, however he was there to work out an alternative.

The Principal was placed in a difficult position. She could support her school staff by sticking to the decision or she could seek another alternative bearing in mind the full circumstances. Laura's father explained the importance of the formal to Laura and how she had been so committed to preparing for the perfect evening. He sought a compassionate response from the Principal.

The late US general Norman Schwarzkopf espoused two rules on leadership. These will be covered in more detail in the Leadership part:

Number One: When placed in command, *take charge*.

Number Two: Do the *right* thing.

Great leaders do both these things consistently. The school Principal made her decision to give Laura an alternative punishment and allow her to attend the formal.

Some of you may not agree with the Principal's decision.

However, she made the decision by doing what she considered to be the right thing. It would have been easy for her to have adhered to the initial decision, which would also have served as a warning to other students who had notions of wagging. Instead the Principal, in her wisdom, chose to overrule in this instance and do the right thing by Laura and her family. The Principal showed compassion.

It takes a strong person to made decisions and stick by the rules. It takes a strong leader to know when to change their decision.

WHY SHOULD SPEAKERS HAVE COMPASSION?

Great speakers demonstrate compassion, no matter what the situation or who the audience is in front of them.

Imagine if you are presenting bad news to an audience. If you do not have compassion, you may come across as aggressive or negative and get your audience offside. At times like this, you need to display empathy.

Good speakers put themselves in their audience's shoes. They try to understand the impact of their message on their audience, and pre-empt their reaction to the bad news. They position their message to show genuine empathy for their audience and try to come up with some kind of win for their audience or provide them with hope for a better outcome.

HOW TO DEVELOP COMPASSION

Some of us are born compassionate. Think of all those selfless volunteers who give of their time and energy for the greater good of their community. Often we are compassionate in times of human suffering. Remember the tsunami that devastated parts of Indonesia and Sri Lanka. Hundreds of thousands of lives lost, homes demolished, carnage everywhere. Millions of Australians and people around the world felt compassion. Donations to suffering victims of the tsunami amounted to millions of dollars. We can be compassionate when we feel a need to help others, either directly or indirectly.

For those of us who do not feel that we are compassionate, the good news is that compassion can be learnt.

We can choose to be compassionate every day. Giving up your seat on the train or bus for an elderly person is an act of compassion. Buying a copy of *The Big Issue* to help the disadvantaged is an act of compassion. Helping a mother carry a pram up the stairs at Central Station is compassionate. There are hundreds of opportunities every day for us to be more compassionate. So, put 'compassion' on your radar. See how many compassionate acts you can perform for a week, starting tomorrow. Start with small compassionate acts. Donate five dollars to a charity; give up your bus seat for an elderly person; volunteer one hour of your time towards a good cause.

Be Gracious

Great speakers care for their audience, whom they believe they are there to serve. They serve their audience by not *preaching* and *instructing*, rather by *connecting*.

Working with many great leaders across industries and from all around the world, I have observed that most of them are gracious. While they can be tough decision makers, they have excellent manners and are gracious hosts. Every once in a while you may come across a leader who is not gracious, and this stands out to their detriment.

THE ARROGANT CEO

A few years ago, I was the MC for a large business forum. There were several high profile speakers on the agenda speaking to an audience of 300 people. My role was to introduce the speakers and also to support any requirements that they had for their presentation. Since we did not have one of those electronic pointers to move from slide to slide, I had arranged for a young man to change the slides at the cue of the presenter.

One of the presenters was the CEO of a well-established IT software company and he had a number of slides for his presentation. He was moving quite quickly through the slides. In the middle of his presentation he simply stopped speaking. He glared at the young man controlling the slideshow and reprimanded him in front of the whole audience: 'Did I ask you to move onto the next slide?' What followed was an embarrassing silence, during which the red-faced young man sheepishly changed the slideshow to the previous slide. The CEO then continued as if nothing had happened. There was no apology from him for his outburst.

While I fondly remember many great presenters and leaders at that forum, I will never forget the unsavoury incident involving that particular CEO.

BE VIGILANT – YOU ARE ALWAYS BEING OBSERVED

As an individual you are always under observation. Your child will observe you as a role model. Your manager will observe you to ensure you are meeting his expectations. A job interviewer will observe you to determine if you are a good fit for her business. As a speaker, you are under even greater scrutiny. From the time you are being introduced by the MC to the time you finish speaking or even afterwards, mingling with the audience, you are being observed.

So be consistent and behave in the way you'd like your audience to remember you.

MEDICAL STUDENTS ADMIRE THE 'CARE' FACTOR

A few years ago, I was invited to run a public-speaking workshop for sixty post-grads from Sydney University's Medical Society. The workshop was scheduled for the end of a three-day program, during which the students were to hear from many distinguished professors, well-known local celebrities and a number of politicians, including future Australian prime minister Tony Abbott. Some of the speakers were famous, and many would have been recognised by most Australians.

I asked the group who they thought was the best speaker of the program. Theirs was a unanimous decision. It was Professor The Hon. Dame Marie Bashir AD CVO, the former NSW governor. I must confess that I was surprised when they mentioned her, as I thought that there were more influential and practised speakers in the line-up. But when they explained their response, I understood perfectly their choice of the governor.

The students told me how impressed they were by the governor's stories of how she used to travel on Sydney's famous Parramatta Road. When she saw homeless people, she would stop her car, step out and talk to them to try to understand their plight. Here was a woman who touched a group of highly intelligent medical students with her compassion and care. How many politicians do you know who would do what Marie Bashir did? In fact, how many people in general do you know who would do that?

Marie Bashir is obviously a caring and genuine person and this authenticity came through to her audience of future medical practitioners whose philosophy is to care for their patients. The lesson we can take away as presenters is to care for our audience, no matter what our message is to them. Care for our audience means firstly understanding who they are, understanding their beliefs and values, considering why they should listen to you. Care for your audience means discovering how you can help them. Your philosophy must be to make the audience's world a slightly better place than before they came to hear you speak.

Summary

How to respect your audience:

1. Before the speech, prepare by understanding who your audience is, what their beliefs are, what values they hold dear and what they are expecting to hear from you.

2. During the presentation check for non-verbal clues to see if you are connecting with the audience, rather than putting them to sleep or confusing them. If that's the case, show respect by taking corrective action.

3. Respect the audience by providing the opportunity for them to ask questions or offer their opinions. Show respect by answering their questions with sincerity.

4. After the presentation, obtain feedback to gauge how your message has been received and how you might improve it.

How to have compassion as a speaker:

1. Great speakers have compassion. Having compassion allows you to see other people's point of view and develop empathy for them. Develop a sense of genuine compassion and you will make a strong connection with your audience.

2. Be gracious. As a speaker know that you are being observed and judged before, during and after your speech. Always display good manners and be vigilant about how you come across to others.

3. If your audience knows that you care, they will reciprocate and return your respect many times over and they will eagerly look forward to your next speech.

PART FOUR
Leadership

Attending my local gym, I made an interesting observation. The 24-hour gym has a number of large tinted windows and there is a line of six treadmills facing these windows. While on the treadmill, I can observe what's going on in the car park. What's more interesting to me is that directly opposite the gym is a McDonald's restaurant as well as a KFC restaurant. No matter what time of day I go to the gym, while on the treadmill I can see cars lining up to get their fix of fast food. And then within the gym, I observe fellow gym members. Each of them is working out to get their body a little fitter and healthier.

It struck me that all of us have choices in life. Some of us choose to eat fast food; others choose to get a little fitter. I have been on both sides of the fence and from time to time will choose either depending on how I feel or what phase I'm going through. However, I know that I have a choice and should live with whatever the consequences of that choice may be. I take full responsibility for it.

Being accountable for your choices is what leadership is about. In this part, we explore elements of what makes a good leader and learn how to apply these to becoming strong speakers. If you want to become a great presenter, then developing leadership qualities is essential. In this part, we will explore the qualities, traits and behaviours of good leaders and learn how to apply these when speaking.

Take Charge

Taking charge is the first step towards behaving like a leader. When you decide to take charge, things begin to change. You begin to take control of all aspects of your life. This chapter outlines the importance of taking responsibility and how you can vastly improve your success as a speaker by taking charge.

Do the Right Thing

Doing the right thing as a speaker is about ensuring that you consider your audience in every respect of your presentation. You will learn how to prepare your message with a win-win philosophy in mind, and about your moral obligation towards your audience.

Challenge Yourself

The focus of this chapter is to explore how to stretch yourself as a person and as a speaker. You will learn how to use SMART objectives as a framework to set yourself stretch objectives and what to do to achieve your stretch goals.

Leverage Opportunities

This chapter considers opportunities, whether in the workplace or in other aspects of life. Opportunities are always present, you just need to know how to spot them, create them, and most importantly, seize them. As a speaker you will learn the value of taking opportunities to present and how this can increase your demand.

Influence Your Audience

Every day, consciously or subconsciously we influence or are being influenced by others. In this chapter, you will learn about Robert Cialdini's six ways to influence people and how these can be used to maximise your impact as a speaker.

Use Persistence to Succeed

We face challenges each day, be they at work or with family or friends. Keeping focused on a bigger goal and persisting until we achieve our goal is what separates success from failure. We will look at how persistence can help you become a better speaker.

Develop a Positive Attitude

Your attitude counts for everything. I believe that if you have a positive outlook on life, your attract positivity and good things happen. You will learn how having a positive attitude as a speaker is paramount to your success in preparing, building and delivering your message.

Be Inspirational

All great leaders inspire others. Learn the three types of inspirational speakers; discover the type of inspirational speaker you aspire to be and then how to brand yourself as an inspirational speaker.

I consider this the most important part of the book. If there is anything you take from this book, let it be these lessons, as they will serve you well for developing leadership skills in life and as a speaker.

CHAPTER 17

Take Charge

*'We can let circumstances rule us, or we can
take charge and rule our lives from within.'*

EARL NIGHTINGALE

More than a decade ago I attended a business conference featuring a number of famous speakers. The program included former Soviet statesman Mikhail Gorbachev, Al 'Chainsaw' Dunlap (a prominent US business leader hired by Australian billionaire Kerry Packer to implement large staff cuts, hence the nickname), and the late US general Norman Schwarzkopf, famous for his leadership in the first war in Iraq.

While most of the presenters were good, for me there was one who was outstanding and that was General Schwarzkopf. Why? Simple. Because he delivered a clear, memorable message outlining two edicts that he lived by. More than a decade on, I can still clearly see him on that platform delivering these edicts with power and clarity.

General Schwarzkopf's Motto

This is what Schwarzkopf said: When *placed in command* there are two things you need to do.

Number one is *take charge.*

Number two is to *do the right thing*.

In this chapter we'll look at the first one: when placed in command, take charge. Are you a 'take charge' person? Do you accept accountability for your actions?

It's Your Accountability

A few years ago, I had an interest in the share market. I remember speaking with many people about what type of shares they invested in, as I wanted to make my fortune through buying and selling shares. One fine day, I received a tip from my wife's hairdresser. She recommended a company that was drilling for coal seam gas as apparently there was an underground supply to support the entire Sydney region for a hundred years. Well, I was excited by this prospect and naively bought some shares in the company without conducting due diligence.

The inevitable happened; the shares dived. I was livid as I watched my investment go lower and lower week after week until I decided to sell at a substantial loss.

What do you think I did next? Yes, I blamed the hairdresser (not to her face of course) for my loss. Not long after, I was reading an investment book about wealth creation and there was a complete chapter devoted to taking full accountability for making investment decisions.

That made me realise I was not taking responsibility for my actions, but attributing blame to someone else for my shares loss. From then on I vowed that if I bought or sold shares, I would take full accountability for my decision. This is a mantra I follow for all of my life decisions: take charge and be fully accountable for all my actions.

Take Charge as a Speaker

So what does taking charge have to do with being a speaker? Everything! Taking full responsibility for everything within your control will ensure that you leave nothing to chance and you don't blame anyone else.

Taking charge starts with the opportunity being presented to you. Once you have an opportunity to speak, here are some areas you can take control over.

SPEAK FIRST ON THE PROGRAM

Your speech may be part of an overall program, so you will need to align to that program. If you can influence the order of speaking, then request to speak earlier in the program. One of the reasons for doing this is that, more often than not, speakers talk for more than their allotted time or the program starts late. Most audiences want the speaking engagement to end on time in order to commence the social part of the occasion or to move on to other engagements. So, the speaker who is last on the program often has less time to deliver his message or must do so to an audience that is tiring or getting bored. Therefore, it may be in your best interest to be one of the earlier speakers, if not first speaker, on the agenda.

There are two other advantages to being first speaker. Firstly, the audience is more inclined to listen to the messages of the first speaker as their interest is piqued at the start. Subsequent speeches may not receive the same attentiveness as speaker number one. The other important advantage is that subsequent speakers may refer to what you have said in their presentations (e.g. 'Earlier, John made a great point when he said …'). This validates you as a speaker and provides free marketing courtesy of other speakers. So, take charge and influence your slot on the program.

If there is a valid reason that you are the last speaker (often the keynote is the last speaker and that is an honour), then speak to the MC to ensure that a tight program is run and you are provided with sufficient time to complete your entire presentation.

However, as Scouts are taught: be prepared. If you are final speaker on the agenda, make sure that you have a shortened version of your message ready to deliver. If your speaking time is reduced, then you are prepared with a short compelling message or even one that is bait for your audience to speak with you post-event.

THE MC IS YOUR ALLY – USE WISELY

You can influence how your speech goes even before you utter the first word. Your audience is sitting in judgment (consciously or unconsciously) from the time they see your name on the program. The first item within your control is to work with the events team or MC to craft an appropriate, short, compelling synopsis of your message that can be added to the flyer. This is your first opportunity to establish credibility with your audience. Your objective is to get the audience excited about your message.

The next opportunity is to work on a carefully crafted introduction about yourself to ensure you are seen as a credible speaker. Provide the introduction to the MC with instructions to read it as is. The introduction should appear as if the MC has written it, so it does not seem that you are the architect of blatant self-promotion. Use this opportunity to outline what you have achieved that directly relates to your message. Remember that the audience is asking 'Who is this speaker? And why should I listen to him?'

If you can establish who you are, what you have achieved and what gives you the right to stand on that platform and take up people's time (that they will never get back), then this introduction becomes a vital part of establishing credibility with your audience. If you are speaking on climate change, for example, then the introduction should include any credible experience you have relating to that topic. You may have three PhDs, but if none of them relate to your message, that information is irrelevant to the audience except to tell them that you are a learned person.

REMEMBER MURPHY'S LAW

We all know Murphy's Law says 'anything that can go wrong will go wrong'. As a leader, remember this law and know that there are things within your control that will put the odds back in your favour.

The first thing to do is to take control of your speech. If you are using speaking notes, make sure you have a hard copy with you. If you are using a PowerPoint presentation, ensure that you provide a soft copy to the MC and also have a backup on a USB stick.

If you are speaking using technology like a microphone and laptop, then ensure all of that is working well beforehand. I always meet the 'sound guy' half an hour before to test the equipment with him and also ask him for sound adjustments so that the acoustics are in my favour. It pays to have a basic understanding of how the equipment works and the fallback plan in case Murphy strikes with his damned law.

Think of all of the risks associated with doing your presentation, and establish a backup plan for each of them. This is a part of good leadership, ensuring that you have appropriate contingencies in place.

Summary

Take charge of your speaking assignment.

1. Speak on the program in the order that best suits your message.

2. Use the MC wisely to establish credibility on your behalf.

3. Check technology and ensure you have a back-up plan in case Murphy strikes.

CHAPTER 18

Do the Right Thing

*'That old law about 'an eye for an eye'
leaves everybody blind. The time is always
right to do the right thing.'*

Martin Luther King, Jr.

At the entrance to the conference rooms of an international consultancy firm, large banners containing inspirational quotes have been strategically placed. One that caught my eye was a quote from J.K. Rowling, world-renowned author of the *Harry Potter* series.

Her simple but powerful thought was *'We have to choose between what is right and what is easy.'*

We humans are not always proactive by nature and if there is an easy way, most of us will take it. J.K. Rowling suggests we do otherwise. In the Tell Stories chapter of this book, I gave an example about a medical emergency on an aeroplane, in which there was one airline staff member who took charge of the situation. His name was Paul and he was second in command after the pilot. What impressed us was how Paul did the right thing to ensure that the sick woman was taken care of. He had one staff member constantly talking and encouraging the woman, a continual pep talk to let her know they were there for her.

Paul also ensured that each of the support crew took breaks. This was a stressful time for all involved and he wanted to make sure they were suitably refreshed and then refocused to support him. He could have kept them working constantly (just as he was) but he chose to do the right thing by them and no wonder they gave him their all. Wow, what a leader; taking charge of the situation and also doing the right thing.

My wife was so impressed by what Paul did, that she wrote to Sir Richard Branson (founder and CEO of Virgin Atlantic) to praise Paul's heroics. I do hope that he was appropriately rewarded for doing his job so well and exhibiting great leadership traits.

What does 'the right thing' mean? Do the right thing by whom? To me, this means considering the impact of your actions on others. Think win-win. Think moral obligation. Let's look at each of these.

Think Win-Win

What is win-win? A win-win is a situation where through cooperation, compromise, or group participation all parties benefit; as opposed to a *win-lose* situation, where one person wins while another loses. The term can be applied to many aspects of daily life.

Do you operate with a win-win mentality? Or do you think you can gain more with a win-lose mindset?

Think of the last time you negotiated something. Perhaps it was negotiating a pay rise with your manager. Did you go in there with a win-win mindset? If you answered yes, then I would assume you had factual evidence of the value you had provided to justify the pay rise. If you did get it, then congratulations – you are indeed thinking win-win.

The tangible value you provided to your company (their win) should be met with a fair salary increase for you (your win). Of course, this situation is in a perfect world. There are many other factors that may come into play. The economic climate or your company's financial situation may influence whether or not you obtain the pay rise, no matter how much value you have added. Your interpretation of providing value may be quite different to your manager's view. Many companies are bound by their human resources policies for pay rises. Within the bounds of such restrictions, you should always seek a win-win situation that is seen as fair by all parties.

THINKING WIN-LOSE

George lives in a majestic home on acreage in the northern suburbs of Sydney. He and his family have done very well out of buying property, renovating it and then selling it for a solid profit. There is nothing wrong with that; it takes imagination, a good plan and hard work to make this possible. George has been doing this for a few years – buying, renovating, selling and repeating the process.

A couple of years ago one of his properties sold for upwards of $3.5 million. Well done, George, all the hard work paid off.

George has created his own success in life and will continue to do so. However, there is another side to George. He has a win-lose attitude.

George constantly brags to me about his financial wins. For all of his wealth, George is always looking for an angle – ways to financially 'win' over others. He brags about how he smashes (figuratively) people into submission. What he does not realise or care about is that every time he wins against someone, they are *losing*. George is only concerned about that next win.

Knowing this, I will never do business with George. Because I know that George will be out to win financially at all costs.

WIN-WIN IS THE WAY TO GO

There is nothing wrong with being frugal or attempting to make more money. But there are two ways to go about it. If you maintain a win-lose philosophy, this will ultimately lead to fewer people wanting to do business with you, being friends with you or trusting you.

The other way is to have a win-win mentality. In all your dealings with others, whether financially or otherwise, always think 'How can we both win?' Ask yourself 'What are the benefits that both the other party and I can get out of this interaction?'

It may be a good idea to check with the other party so that they can validate the benefits to both of you. They may come up with additional benefits that you have not thought about. Two heads are always better than one. People want to do business with others when they know that the other person has their interest at heart too. A win-win philosophy will help build trust, build better relationships and a stronger outcome for all.

Think Win-Win as a Speaker

How can we apply the win-win philosophy as a speaker? We want a win for you as a speaker and for the audience as well.

PROVIDE VALUE

One way to achieve a win-win is to focus on the value you provide to your audience. This will lead to a win for your audience. So, how do you win? You win through establishing or enhancing your credibility. The more value you provide through your message, the more you will be seen as a credible person. When crafting your message, ask yourself what can your listeners learn from it? What can they apply to their daily lives? What will be the takeaway from your speech? All of these answers should form the core of your message and you can then work backwards to develop the speech to ensure that it is a win-win.

RESPECT YOUR AUDIENCE'S VALUES

As discussed in Chapter 16, Care For Your Audience, you will be doing the right thing by your listeners if you understand their values. Find out what their stance is likely to be on contentious issues such as feminism or positive discrimination, and tread carefully in those areas. You don't have to agree with them, you may even be trying to convince them otherwise, but do not disparage. One method of obtaining an understanding of your audience's values is to conduct a straw poll prior to preparing your speech. Respecting your listeners will mean they respect you in return.

MORAL OBLIGATION AS A SPEAKER

'Doing the right thing' implies a moral obligation, and your moral obligation as a speaker is to be honest. Being honest means presenting information that is based on facts. We all have opinions, but when your message is based on facts there are advantages for both you and the audience. You increase your credibility by showing that you have taken the time to conduct thorough research and present information that is authoritative. The audience has the benefit of being able to rely on the information and facts presented for their own purposes.

Summary

1. Doing the right thing as a speaker is about ensuring that you consider your audience in every part of your presentation. Preparing your message with a win-win philosophy in mind will drive you towards a positive outcome for your audience.

2. Win-win techniques for speakers include providing value, respecting your audience's values and basing your speech on facts not opinion.

CHAPTER 19

Challenge Yourself

'I like the challenge of trying different things and wondering whether it's going to work or whether I'm going to fall flat on my face.'

JOHNNY DEPP

Most corporations ensure that their employees set annual objectives to help achieve business goals. These objectives are often set using the SMART acronym.

SMART objectives mean:

S (specific – the objectives are clear and specific)

M (measurable – the objectives have tangible measures)

A (attainable – the objectives are within the capability of the employee)

R (relevant – the objectives are relevant to the employee's job)

T (time-bound – the objectives have a time-frame within which to be achieved)

Many corporations are now asking employees to add 'stretch' objectives. A stretch objective is exactly what it sounds like; it's requiring the employee to stretch beyond their current capabilities.

SMART objectives are set to be attainable and within the capabilities of the employee. Stretch objectives are set beyond the current capabilities of the employee. The employee is expected to increase their skills to meet the stretch objective.

An example of a stretch objective is where a sales person is asked to make 10% more sales than their normal objective. There may be a financial incentive attached to meeting the stretch objective. So, the goal is that the sales person will develop a plan and execute it to enable them to meet their stretch objective. This may mean increasing the number of people they sell to, learning new sales techniques, or looking at creative ways to make more sales.

Have you been given stretch objectives? Did you have a plan to achieve these objectives? How did you act on this plan? Did you succeed in achieving your stretch objectives? To increase your leadership capabilities, see if you can incorporate stretch objectives into what you want to achieve. This way you will be constantly seeking ways to grow as an individual.

The Four-Minute Mile

One person who challenged himself was Sir Roger Bannister, the famous English athlete best known for running the first sub-four-minute mile.

Prior to achieving this goal, Bannister competed in the 1952 Helsinki Olympic Games.

In the Olympic Games semi-finals of the 1500m, Bannister's confidence took a blow when he finished fifth, just narrowly qualifying for the final. The 1500m final was another massive disappointment for Bannister as he could only muster fourth place.

The Olympic Games failure was reflection time for Bannister. He eventually decided to set himself a new challenge: to be the first person to run a sub-4 minute mile.

He intensified his training until he felt ready. History now shows that the race in May 1954 at Oxford proved to be memorable with Bannister finally reaching his dream with a time of 3 min 59.4 sec.

There are some important lessons we can learn from Sir Roger Bannister's record.

BELIEF

First, when you challenge yourself, believe that it *can* be accomplished. According to Bannister, he always believed that the four-minute mile was possible. Many others believed it was impossible. Interestingly, the record lasted only 46 days until Australian John Landy beat Bannister's time. It's interesting because once Bannister broke the record, others started to believe it was possible, and achieved what was previously thought by many to be unachievable.

Belief is vital; the saying *'what the mind believes, it can achieve'* is very true. So, whatever challenge you set yourself, believe with all your intensity that it is possible and then do what Bannister did next.

TAKE BABY STEPS

Bannister carefully planned his way towards achieving his goal. He prepared for specific races and set smaller goals to ready himself for the ultimate prize. Follow his lead by working towards larger goals, first breaking them down into monthly or even weekly targets. By setting smaller, achievable targets, you are more likely to stay motivated. Be sure to congratulate and treat yourself when you reach those targets.

My initial goal in writing this book was to complete it within one year. However due to many self-imposed distractions, the completion of the book took seven years. The best traction I got was when I met a work colleague, Simon Lenz, who was developing his own brand and line of audio products. Simon is one of the most focused people I have met. He had a clear end game and diligently wrote fortnightly actions towards his goal, taking great pleasure in crossing off each task. Meticulously completing each task set Simon up to succeed in developing his product.

Simon provided encouragement and a roadmap of how I could take daily and weekly steps to research and write pages for this book. I developed a habit of doing something to create this book almost every day. It took baby steps at first but finally I achieved what I set out to do.

Everyone can do this with a little planning and commitment. Set yourself a specific challenge, plan for how you will achieve the goal over a certain period of time and get into the habit of taking action on a regular basis that will progress you towards the greater goal.

SETBACKS

There will always be setbacks on your way to achieving your goal.

Bannister had many setbacks and one that really discouraged him was the Olympic Games failure. But as many champions do, he learnt from the experience, dusted himself off and with great tenacity moved towards his goal. Inspirational! The lesson from Bannister is to learn from mistakes, don't be discouraged, and keep moving towards the ultimate goal.

Importantly, it's our reaction to the setback that will make or break us. We may choose to give up and say it's too hard. Or we may delay until another time. Or, we may persevere like Bannister did.

Andrew's Achievement

Stuttering or stammering is a speech disorder which makes it difficult for the stutterer to get sounds out clearly. When I first met Andrew, he was a fellow competitor during a public-speaking competition. During his contest speech, Andrew often stuttered but completed his speech, to the delight of the audience.

After the contest I spoke with Andrew who informed me that he had stuttered all of his life but aimed to overcome this challenge through public speaking. Not only did Andrew want to overcome the problem, but he wanted to ultimately compete at the highest level of public-speaking competition. What a *magnificent challenge* he had set himself!

Over the years, I observed Andrew's confidence increase and his stuttering reduce dramatically. This was achieved through great determination. Andrew was constantly on the lookout for opportunities to present and to compete in speaking contests. He did have setbacks along the way, including one occasion in a speech contest when his stuttering got so bad that he had to stop and in great embarrassment shuffle off the platform.

Did that setback stop him? It may have done many others, but not Andrew!

Andrew focused on his ultimate mission and continually took every opportunity to overcome his speech disorder. In the end, Andrew did achieve success by placing in one of the public-speaking contests at state level. What an achievement!

Speaking Challenges

Whatever your speaking capability, set yourself a stretch goal to improve dramatically. Stretch goals are best achieved by taking baby steps and then increasing the momentum as you become more confident.

For example, you may be comfortable presenting to three or four people. You could have a stretch goal to present to 100 people within one year. A first step to achieving this may be to prepare to present to a group of 10 initially. Then a month later you could aim to present to a group of 20. And so on, until you have achieved your goal of presenting to 100 people. Of course, you have to remember that meeting 100 people's expectations may be quite different to meeting the expectations of three people. You'll need to ensure that there is great value in your message to 100 people.

Your challenge as a speaker may be presenting to senior management or executives. This will again require you to do your homework and prepare appropriately for this audience. Or your stretch goal may be to become an expert in a subject that you currently have very little knowledge on. Once you have obtained in-depth knowledge you may claim to be an authority on the topic and present a message of value to others.

Whatever your stretch goal as a speaker, develop a plan that charts how you will reach your final goal, just like Sir Roger Bannister and Andrew did. Take baby steps to achieve your ultimate prize and go for it!

Summary

1. Use SMART objectives as a framework to set yourself stretch objectives.

2. Believe in yourself and know that you will be capable of achieving your stretch goals.

3. Prepare a plan that includes baby steps and increase the challenges until you achieve your stretch goal.

4. Don't be discouraged by setbacks. Most big successes come after setbacks. It's how you deal with the setbacks that will determine your success. Learn from them and move forward.

5. Keep your eyes on the ultimate prize and you will eventually get there.

CHAPTER 20

Leverage Opportunities

*'To hell with circumstances,
I create opportunities.'*

BRUCE LEE

Acres of Diamonds

Dr. Russell Conwell was an American Baptist minister who inspired his audiences with the 'Acres of Diamonds' story.

The story is about a farmer, Al Hafed, living a contented life on the banks of the River Indus. One day he was visited by a priest who told him about all the riches the world held including diamonds that would make him rich beyond his wildest dreams. Al-Hafed decided that he wasn't satisfied with his life after all and wanted more. So, he sold his farm and went travelling in search of diamonds across Persia and Europe. Unfortunately Al-Hafed did not find any diamonds and died penniless.

The story continues that the man who had bought Al-Hafed's farm was bathing his animals in the stream one fine day when he noticed a shimmering glint. It was a diamond. On excavating the farm he discovered one of the largest diamond mines in the world.

(Note: the Acres of Diamonds story is available on the Internet for free. It is a short story and a good read. I encourage you to read it and obtain your own insights from this story).

LESSON FROM ACRES OF DIAMONDS

The key lesson we can take from Cornwell's story is to look within yourself and your immediate circumstances to discover your fortune.

Look Within Yourself

A few years ago, I too wanted to be successful. I dreamed up many harebrained business schemes to achieve my fortune. Schemes like creating a board game similar to Scrabble. I knew nothing about creating a board game and that's where the dream ended. Then I came across the Acres of Diamonds story. It made me reflect on what I was doing and how I was venturing off the path to find success. I realised that I needed to look within, look at my capabilities, skills, experiences and talents. I finally discovered that I wanted to help others overcome their fear of speaking and transform into confident speakers.

This was within my capabilities, having learnt many speaking strategies and applied them in real life before thousands of people. With many successes and failures behind me, I learnt the lessons that I can now share with you in this book.

What are you skills and capabilities? What experiences have

you had that you can use to become an expert in a particular field or apply to a business or job? One action that worked for me was to jot down all of my skills, capabilities and experiences. This helped me to assess what I was capable of and where to focus my attention. I encourage you to do the same and conduct a self-assessment of the possibilities where you can provide value to others.

Opportunities as a Speaker

You will find that there are many opportunities for you as a speaker. Let's first look at available opportunities.

As you will recall from the Structure part, as long as you have a message that is one of the following then there will always be opportunities:

- An informative message that provides educational value for your audience;

- An influential message that moves your audience to do something different;

- An inspirational message that stimulates your audience to greater heights.

USE EXISTING OPPORTUNITIES

Once you have a particular message that fits one of the above purposes it will be easy to find your audience. Depending on your message, your audience may be work colleagues, business people, customers, not-for-profit organisations, family or friends.

If an opportunity presents itself, seize it!

Look for existing meetings that you already attend for

an opportunity to speak. Since these meetings are already established, all you do is contact the organiser and get on the program. For example, if you want to present to work colleagues, then establish if there is a regular meeting where you can share your message. Make sure that your message aligns in some way to the overall objective of the meeting.

If you find it difficult to obtain a ready-made audience, then, as mentioned in the Confidence part, consider joining a public-speaking organisation to present and practise your speech. Otherwise, go to plan B and create an opportunity.

CREATE OPPORTUNITIES

Most of us will go down the path of only responding to existing opportunities. However if there are no available opportunities, what do we do? Should we wait for an opportunity to surface or should we create our own opportunities?

Creating opportunities is challenging as it means that we may need to venture into new territory or spend time to develop the opportunity. But what if the opportunity provided a massive benefit? Would it not be worthwhile?

To establish whether or not an opportunity is worthwhile you need to perform a cost-benefit analysis. This would mean comparing the cost of developing the opportunity (time, effort, dollars) versus the benefits (tangible, intangible, goodwill). If you assess that the benefits outweigh the cost, by all means pursue the creation of the new opportunity.

Woodchopping 101

A friend of mine, Greg, is a competitive woodchopper. He is quite successful at this and often competes at the annual Easter

Show in Sydney. Greg approached me for my thoughts on how he could present to a bunch of young men interested in the sport. Greg saw this as an opportunity to entice youngsters to be involved in the sport and through his demonstrations teach them 'Woodchopping 101'.

Greg and I worked through a plan of firstly assessing if there was sufficient interest from young men for the sport. We spoke with a couple of them to confirm specifically what would interest them. Greg shared some techniques with the two boys and then decided what would work with the larger group.

Greg invited the larger group to a hands-on workshop where he related how he got started in woodchopping and included some humorous anecdotes about woodchopping competitions. He then demonstrated some of the basics of woodchopping and invited questions. Everyone in the audience was then invited to come up and participate in a woodchopping activity with Greg expertly overseeing them.

Greg had created an opportunity for these young lads to learn and enjoy an art that was dear to him.

If there are no foreseeable opportunities for you to deliver your message, can you create one? You do not have to present to a large audience. It could be to two or three people. As long as your message has some value, like Greg's *woodchopping 101* workshops, then go ahead and create the opportunity to present your message.

Summary

1. Learn the great lessons from the Acres of Diamonds story and look within yourself, at your skills and experiences for opportunities to succeed.

2. If an opportunity presents itself, seize it! Look for opportunities as a speaker where you can present your message. Ensure your message has one or more of these purposes: to be informative, influential or inspirational.

3. To practise your message, consider joining a public-speaking group. This way you will have a captive audience who can provide you with friendly feedback on your message.

4. If there are no obvious opportunities to present your message, create your own. Think about the value that you can provide to an audience and look at options for how you can create an event to present your message.

CHAPTER 21

Influence Your Audience

*'No-one can make you feel
inferior without your consent.'*

Eleanor Roosevelt

At the start of an 18-day coach tour around Spain, our tour director (TD) suggested a number of paid optional experiences that we could do. These optional experiences were in addition to the normal itinerary and included a hosted dinner with a local family, a traditional folkloric show, and cruising around the harbour. As the time approached for each optional experience, the TD would request confirmation of numbers, always stating 'If we do not get x number of people, the optional experience will be cancelled.' I found this tactic an interesting way for the TD to influence the outcome. He left it to those who definitely wanted to go to possibly influence their fellow travellers to make up the required numbers.

This is an example of how each and every day we influence or are influenced by others. You may attempt to influence someone at work to act in a certain way, or do something for you. Or your partner may influence you to attend a dinner with your in-laws.

Social Influence

What is influence? There are many types of influence but I will limit this chapter to social influence. Social influence is generally described as the persuasive effect we have on one another with regard to emotions, opinions, or behaviours.

The different types of social influence are captured in an excellent book, *Influence: the Psychology of Persuasion,* by Robert Cialdini. The book provides the reader with six areas of influence to become aware of so that we can influence others or prevent being influenced by others. Let's look at each of the six areas and then how we can apply them as a speaker.

RECIPROCITY

As humans, we generally aim to return favours, pay back debts, and treat others as they treat us. According to Cialdini's view on reciprocity, this can lead us to feel obliged to pay others back if they have done something for us. This is because we feel indebted to them. For example, if a colleague helps you when you're busy preparing for an important meeting, you may feel obliged to support him with a project he is working on.

Some marketers offer free material to potential customers, such as a newsletter or a sample of their product. They are hoping that this will lead to reciprocation and you will buy more of their products or use their services.

COMMITMENT (AND CONSISTENCY)

Cialdini says that we have a deep desire to be consistent. For this reason, once we've committed to something, we're then more inclined to go through with it.

For instance, you'd probably be more likely to support a change if you were involved early and asked to share your ideas and thoughts.

SOCIAL PROOF

This principle relies on people's sense of 'safety in numbers'. For example, we're more likely to come in early to work if everyone in the team is doing the same. The assumption is that if others are doing something, then it must be the right way.

LIKEABILITY

This principle states that we're more likely to be influenced by people we like. Likeability comes in many forms – people may be similar or familiar to us, they may compliment us, or we may simply trust them.

People are more likely to buy from people like themselves, from friends, and from people they know and respect. This is a tactic used with great success by network marketing businesses who encourage their sales staff to target the low hanging fruit first: friends and family.

AUTHORITY

We feel a sense of duty or obligation to people in positions of authority. This is why advertisers of pharmaceutical products employ doctors as advocates for their marketing or toothpaste companies hire dentists to sell their products. It's also why most of us will do what our manager requests of us.

Job titles, uniforms and even accessories like cars or gadgets can lend an air of authority, and can persuade us to accept what people in authority say.

SCARCITY

This principle says that things are more attractive when their availability is restricted, or when we stand to lose the opportunity to acquire them on favourable terms. For instance, we might buy something immediately if we're told that it's the last one, or that a special offer will soon expire.

Influencing people can have a direct or indirect benefit for us. As discussed earlier in the section on win-win in Chapter 18, Do the Right Thing, it is important to provide some benefit to the person that you are attempting to influence. That way, you both win. So, keep that in mind when you are attempting to influence.

Ask yourself, what can the person I am trying to influence gain? Then, what can I gain by attempting to influence them? If you honestly believe that there is a benefit for both of you, then go ahead and influence them.

How Can You Use These Influencing Skills as a Speaker?

When you are preparing a speech, consider that you will often be required to influence your audience. You may want your audience to take action in the form of volunteering their time, donating generously to a worthy cause, or adopting the new technology you are advocating. How you influence will depend on your ability, your audience and the outcomes you expect from your message.

Please be ethical when you use any of these strategies, as your good reputation should be maintained first and foremost. A good way to do this is to make sure that you are being honest and using facts when employing influencing techniques.

Let's review each of these influencing strategies to see where you can leverage them as a speaker.

RECIPROCITY

Some motivational speakers employ the reciprocation technique very effectively. They offer a free event that provides some value to the audience (this is the 'hook'). While they provide you with some information that may be of value to you, their strategy is to get you to book into their three, five or seven-day seminar. But that's how the law of reciprocity works. Do something for others and they will reciprocate.

During a championship speaking competition, a contestant was speaking about his travels to China. He spoke of how the Chinese loved their fortune cookies. At this point he produced from a bag a number of individually wrapped fortune cookies and proceeded to throw them to the audience randomly. Those who caught the fortune cookies appeared delighted to have received a 'prize'. Giving away freebies to your audience is a great way to encourage them to reciprocate in some way (perhaps give you a standing ovation or be an advocate for you as a speaker).

As a speaker, think about how you can leverage the law of reciprocity. Think about what you can give your audience that they can benefit from, perhaps it is freebies, or how about a simple one-page handout of your key messages that they can take home?

I have sometimes produced a summary of key thoughts and included them on a business-card-sized card that the audience could use for quick reference. Feedback indicates that they love the card and see it as good value.

If you are generous, you could provide services free of charge. For example, if you are selling training workshops to improve PC skills, you may want to offer some free training with a view to obtaining more business down the track. Companies receiving the free training may reciprocate by sending staff to your paid training sessions.

Consider the rule of reciprocity as a means to influence your audience and hopefully they may reciprocate in some way.

COMMITMENT (AND CONSISTENCY)

As a speaker you can use the commitment principle to influence your audience in the following ways:

Show Me the Money

That famous line from the movie *Jerry Maguire* (starring Tom Cruise) essentially asks 'what's in it for me?' It says if you want something, then show me what I'll get out of it before I sign up. If you want commitment from your audience, justify how they can benefit from what you are asking them to do.

For example, if you want your audience to volunteer their services at Salvation Army stores, then how could you get them to commit? One way is to get a current volunteer to espouse the benefits of being a volunteer: a sense of community, making new friends, a sense of purpose and the satisfaction of helping those less advantaged than yourself. The feel-good factor is a strong motivator and helps to build commitment.

Another way to obtain commitment from your audience may be to get them involved from the start using the same example of volunteering their services at the Salvation Army, ask their input about the benefits to them for volunteering and jot these ideas on a whiteboard they can visually see the benefits they have identified and hopefully commit to a worthy cause of volunteering their services.

SOCIAL PROOF

As a speaker, you can use social proof by providing evidence of how people, preferably experts or well-known people, have adopted what you are selling with a view to influencing your audience to buy your product or service.

For example, if you are presenting to your audience on a new technology, you may want to research who else has benefited from using it. This may require time to research, but it will be time well spent. If you can convince your audience of the strong *demand* for your product, especially from credible people, it will increase the odds of being influenced by social proof, i.e. 'if experts or famous people are buying this new service, then it must be good and I should buy it too'.

LIKEABILITY

Likeability will be an important factor in whether or not the audience 'buys' your message. If you are likeable, and the audience can relate to you in some way, you probably have a better chance of influencing them. Conversely if your audience does not like you, they will consciously or subconsciously view your ideas critically and possibly negatively. So, it is imperative that you think about how to make your audience like you.

One of the most common techniques good speakers use is to connect with their audiences by finding some common ground between themselves and the audience.

I remember on one occasion during a technical presentation, a salesperson from interstate commenced his speech by saying how he always loved coming to Sydney (where the presentation was being held) because it was such a vibrant city with spectacular beaches and world-class icons like the Harbour Bridge and Opera House. The audience was primarily made up of Sydneysiders, who would have felt proud of their city and felt an immediate affinity with someone who also admired it.

As a speaker, you need to find out who your audience is. What is this group expecting from you? These expectations will largely determine how you proceed in your plan to make them like you. Will it be your sense of humour? Or your ability to massage their egos? Or how you speak with humility?

Find out as much as you can about your audience and consider what you can do to make them like you.

AUTHORITY

Your job title, what car you drive and even what you wear can make a big difference to how others perceive you.

A few years ago, I consulted to NSW Fire Brigades' training division. This division offered training workshops and events for businesses to help them with fire-hazard precautions. I clearly remember the superintendent of the division informing me that the one major advantage they had against competitors was the

NSW Fire Brigades uniform. He said when clients see training personnel arrive wearing their uniform, they instantly see them as the experts and want to be trained by them.

I saw evidence of this when working with another client: NRMA Motoring Services (NMS). The main business of this company is to provide members with support when their cars break down. I have personally experienced the service of the NMS, and I always have a sense of confidence when I see them arrive that my problem will be resolved with a minimum of fuss and always with a smile. Now, that is service!

They have now started leveraging their brand in a very clever way by establishing large garages to fix and maintain cars. Their customer base is growing because of this. Many people in NSW and the ACT see NMS as the authority, and have confidence in this company's ability to do a good job fixing or maintaining their car.

As a speaker, how can you use authority to influence people? NSW Fire Brigades (now known as Fire and Rescue NSW) and NMS have both built great brands around their ability to resolve customer's problems in their particular sphere of expertise. Customers in NSW know that if they want fire safety training that the authority on the subject is the NSW Fire Brigades. The people of NSW and ACT know that if they want their car fixed, the experts will do this. NRMA Motoring Services!

Are you an authority on a particular product, service or topic that will help resolve a problem for people? If you are, then congratulations! Use this authority to influence people to obtain more knowledge about your offering, or buy your product.

If you are not currently an authority on the product or service that you are advocating, then decide to become one. Learn everything you can about the subject and arm yourself with facts from creditable sources.

As a speaker you are far more likely to influence others if you are a leading authority. If you are just another speaker, the audience will ask 'so what?' If you are the authority, the audience will say 'I want to hear this expert speak!'

SCARCITY

The 2000 Sydney Olympic Games were an exciting time for most Australians. There was an amazing buzz in the city of Sydney and I have never seen so many people happy and excited as during the Games. It was also an opportunity to fundraise for some great causes. Large organisations got on the fundraising bandwagon, and in the spirit of generosity, Australians gave plenty.

I remember attending a corporate function where the team manager had a number of items for auction. He did a great job auctioning off Olympic pins and various Games-related items. The final two items for auction were identical; a leather-covered box containing eight pictures of the current Australian Olympic representatives, such as Ian Thorpe, each on its own square-shaped pin. This was a great auction item and the auctioneer did his best to cajole the audience to bid higher and higher for the first box. The final bid for the first box was $50.

Then the auctioneer held up the second box and said 'Ladies and Gentlemen, this is the final auction item. This box is exactly like the previous one auctioned, except that this box is the absolute final one made in production. There are no more boxes like this and it would make a fantastic memento for whoever is lucky enough to get it. So, let the bidding begin ...'

The bidding began and continued at a furious pace. Soon $50 was outbid, and then $100 and so on until the final bid was $300! An amazing six times more than the previous successful bidder paid for exactly the same item. Six times! Why?

It was simply because the auctioneer did a successful job, sowing the seed of scarcity in the audience's minds, and that paid off handsomely.

Can you as a speaker create an environment of scarcity? There are opportunities to do this. It depends on what it is you are trying to achieve with your audience. For example, if you want to sell a book to your audience, you could create scarcity by offering the first 20 buyers of the book a 50% discount. After those first 20 are sold, the rest are to be offered at full price. If your audience see good value with your offering, then your offer will be snapped up quickly.

Another strategy could be to make your offer time-bound. For example, if you are promoting training for a new system, you could offer face-to-face training, but only for the next two days. After that, training would be made available online with support material. If people see the face-to-face option as more valuable, then they will avail themselves of your good offer.

As a speaker who is offering a deal, consider the following:

- Excite people – always endeavour to make the offering enticing. People are more likely to take up your offering if they are excited about the perceived value.

- Focus on the benefits rather than the features of the offering – Sales 101 training will teach you to always focus on the benefits. For example, someone selling island holidays will succeed by emphasising how *relaxed* you will feel in that environment, how *pampered* you will be by the service and how *satisfied* you will be with the scrumptious food and exotic cocktails.

- Make it scarce – make your offering scarce by making it time-bound or very limited in quantity.

Summary

As a speaker, your influencing skills are vital to how you sell your personal brand and offering. Consider the following when preparing messages for your audience:

1. Use the Reciprocity principle by establishing a free offering for your audience. This could be as simple as a one-page handout summarising the key points of your message or as elaborate as a free training package worth thousands of dollars. With this rule, you are expecting your audience will feel compelled to reciprocate at a later stage.

2. Use the Commitment principle. If you want commitment from your audience, show

them how they can benefit from whatever you are asking them to do.

3. Use the Social Proof principle by providing compelling evidence about how other people have adopted whatever you are selling so that you can convincingly sell the concept to your audience.

4. With the Likeability principle, ask yourself what will make you more likeable to your audience. Will it be your sense of humour, or massaging the audience's ego? Think about what factors can help you become more likeable and use this to your advantage. The audience is more likely to 'buy' if they like you.

5. The Authority principle can be used when you are an expert on a particular product or service that will help people resolve their problems. Work towards becoming an expert, as your audience is far more likely to listen to an authority.

6. Use the Scarcity principle by making

your offer 'scarce' – make it time-bound or limited in quantity. Make sure you get people excited about your offering and always focus on the benefits rather than the features.

CHAPTER 22

Use Persistence to Succeed

'It's hard to beat a person who never gives up.'

BABE RUTH

Babe Ruth is considered one of the all-time greats of baseball in the US, and he strongly advocated tenacity and personal resilience as these were key ingredients in his success.

We all have our fair share of challenges. At times it feels that no matter how hard you try, all your efforts appear to be in vain. Don't despair, for some of life's greatest victories have come to those who have persisted despite the conditions facing them. Success is often achieved through a series of setbacks and dead ends.

The journey towards your goals often defines you as a person, more than the goal that you set out to achieve. Many successful people will confirm that it was the journey, not the fulfilment of the goal, that was most satisfying.

What is Persistence?

Persistence means trying again and again despite apparent failure. This is the hallmark of success for many leaders. Keeping focused on a bigger goal and persisting until we achieve is what separates success from failure.

History abounds with success stories that only eventuated through persistence. One example is Thomas Edison, who overcame repeated setbacks and failures to discover the light bulb. It is reported that it took him no less than 1000 attempts to create what is regarded as one of history's greatest inventions. Following are two more inspirational stories about the power of persistence.

THE LEGEND OF BILLY MILLS

I once presented a speech on persistence and told the story of Billy Mills, an American who overcame many hurdles to cause one of the great upsets in Olympic Games history. Mills was raised on the impoverished Pine Ridge Indian Reservation in South Dakota and orphaned when he was twelve years old. Mills had mixed blood; one parent being native American and the other white, and hence he encountered racial vilification from both sides. The native Americans considered him white, and the whites considered him Indian.

Mills felt alone and alienated from others throughout his youth.

Mills overcame his difficult beginnings by taking up long-distance running. He won cross-country races and qualified to represent the USA in the 1964 Tokyo Olympic Games in the 10,000m race.

The favourite for the 10,000m race was Australia's Ron Clarke, who held the world record. Mills was a virtual unknown and his time in the preliminaries was one minute slower than Clarke's.

Bang! The race was tight and in the backstretch of the final lap Mills appeared to be too far back to be in contention. But with an incredible burst of speed Mills flew past Clarke and crossed the line first! Brilliant!

His Olympic Games record winning time was almost 50 seconds faster than he had run before. Mills had overcome great odds throughout his life and through sheer hard work, belief and persistence finally won the glory all Olympians seek: a gold medal.

Mills' story was an inspiration to me and I'm sure to many thousands of others. There are many similar stories of people in all walks of life who keep persisting until they succeed. One of the greatest traits one can have is to have persistence. We all encounter roadblocks, problems, challenges along life's journey. We have a choice: we can just give up and hope the challenge will go away or we can persist and try to find a solution to pave the way for success.

NEVER GIVE UP! WINSTON CHURCHILL

In 1941, in an episode that has become legend, British prime minister Winston Churchill visited Harrow School to hear the traditional songs he had sung there as a youth. When he was invited to give a speech, Churchill stood before the students and said, more or less, *'Never, never, never, never, never, give up. Never give up. Never give up. Never give up.'*

The common belief that this was the full extent of his speech is incorrect, but it is the section that has resonated ever afterwards in the popular imagination, demonstrating the wisdom of this great man's inspirational words.

Persistence as a Speaker

Becoming a good speaker will require you to overcome challenges as they surface. This will start from the moment you decide you want to be a good speaker and continue throughout your journey to becoming an outstanding presenter.

EARLY DAYS

You'll especially need to persist in your early days as a speaker, as you will have your training wheels on. There will probably be many mistakes that you will make. These mistakes may cause you to become fearful of speaking in future or make you feel like it's all too hard.

I have been there many a time in the early days of speaking at team meetings or presenting to groups. I initially shied away from speaking assignments until I realised that I could no longer hide if I wanted a successful career. So, I started to persist and this changed my philosophy. I decided to learn from every speaking experience. That shift in attitude slowly helped me to gain confidence and develop into a much-improved speaker.

If you are in the early stages of presenting to groups, remember Sir Winston Churchill's famous words and never, ever, ever give up.

PERSISTENCE IN DEVELOPING A STRONG MESSAGE

Your mission to provide value to your audience is paramount to your speaking success. There will be times when you are unsure that the message you have provides value to your audience. Persistence is the elixir for removing doubt. Keep focusing on helping your audience by providing value.

Once you have developed and presented your speech, persistence will pay off if you keep learning from your experience. Here are some ways in which persistence will pay off for you as a presenter.

Refining Your Message

- Obtain feedback on your presentation's content and keep refining your message.

- Self-reflection will help you to improve your message. Can you change words to make them more action oriented or more impressive or help create word pictures in your audience's minds? Add or modify main points to provide your audience with more value.

Presenting Your Message

- Again, obtaining feedback from others will help. Accept all types of feedback, however only act on feedback that enhances your message.

- Self-evaluate and reflect on opportunities to improve your delivery. This may be by using powerful body language, or improving your eye contact with the audience.

Connecting with Your Audience

- There are always opportunities to improve the way you connect with your audience. Persistence will help. Perhaps you can embellish the story you told during your presentation, or tell a story that resonates better.

- You may want to change the way you want your audience to feel. Think about the emotions you want them to feel and modify your message to trigger those emotions.

- Look for additional opportunities to add humour to your message.

Summary

1. Early days as a speaker – persistence as a novice speaker will pay dividends as you overcome challenges. Know that, through persistence, you will be on the road to becoming a strong presenter.

2. Refining your message – through feedback from others and self-reflection, look for opportunities for how you can refine your message so it is better and of greater value to your audience.

3. Presenting your message – self-evaluation

and feedback from others will help you understand how others perceive you. Act on feedback where you think it will enhance how you present in future.

4. Connecting with your audience – connect better with your audience by telling a better story or improving anecdotes. Consider what emotions you want the audience to experience; or add humour to improve how you connect with them.

CHAPTER 23

Develop a Positive Attitude

*'Attitude is a little thing that
makes a big difference.'*

Sir Winston Churchill

Camping isn't my favourite pastime. I've always been a city boy and the thought of roughing it among creatures great and small just does not appeal to me. So, when my wife 'volunteered' me to spend a day camping with my son Josh as part of a school challenge, I tried to find any excuse to get out of participating. However, all my 'but this' and 'but thats' fell on deaf ears. She expertly used the guilt trip: 'Just think, you'll have a great time bonding with Josh'. I finally succumbed. Then she very casually added, 'Oh, and you'll be canoeing with him too'.

Canoeing? Water?!

I strongly objected, 'But, I can't swim. What if I fall in?' (Yes, I can be so wimpy sometimes).

'You'll be fine, you'll have a safety vest on,' she assured me. I wasn't entirely convinced and as the day loomed, I dreaded this whole camping thing.

My son spent a couple of days camping before the father-son day arrived. As I drove to the site to meet Josh, I was filled with negative thoughts. Mosquitoes, yucky food, cramped sleeping conditions, canoeing, drowning (even with a safety vest on).

It started off well as I met the other fathers, and later the boys prepared us a campfire meal of delicious spaghetti bolognese. After dinner, everyone sat in a circle and the main guide, George, proceeded to inform the fathers about the first time he met the boys. At this meeting he asked what their preconceived ideas were about the camp. Most of the campers had heard about the camp from the previous week's attendees, who had many negative comments about their camping experience.

Our sons had come to the camp with negative preconceptions about how boring it was going to be. George then commenced a discussion with the boys about *attitude*. He said that it was up to them and the camp directors to make this a fun, challenging and enjoyable experience. The boys agreed to keep open minds and over the next couple of days, with the support of their camp directors, the boys had some wonderful experiences that they shared with all of us at the campfire that evening.

I was impressed with the way George managed to change the boys' perception of the camp. George made them think about their preconceived notions and asked them to change their attitude to a positive one. This reframing of their expectations totally changed their perception and from that point on they started to look forward to the experience as fun and exciting.

Hearing how George changed their perception made me reflect on how negative I myself felt about the camping experience. I realised if I continued to feel negative then this would possibly affect Josh. Immediately I decided to see the camping experience as positive, spending time with Josh having fun.

What a terrific weekend it turned out to be. Josh and I were the slowest father-son canoeists, but managed to stay out of the water. It was actually quite an exhilarating experience. Importantly I learnt that a positive attitude goes a long way towards being successful.

Are you a positive person? Do you see sunlight rather than clouds? Each morning, do you look forward to the day or do you think *here comes another boring or bad day?*

If you are a 'glass half empty' person, then I encourage you to start thinking positively. Change your attitude to positive. This will lead to positive actions and positive results.

The Tale of Two Teachers

Thinking back to my high school days in a Catholic school there are two teachers I remember most. One was a nun, the late Sister Mary Francis, who was probably one of the most positive influences on me while growing up. She had a wonderful teaching manner; always encouraging her students and being very patient especially with those who were experiencing learning difficulties. She never spoke ill of others and tried to look at every situation in such a way as to make it a positive experience for all. What a great attitude, and she truly was a wonderful human being.

The other teacher I remember was a Brother. But I remember him as being almost exactly the opposite of Sister Mary Francis. He had a pompous attitude and always wanted to be seen as right. I remember him on one occasion asking me to stand up in front of the class and answer a question on chemistry. When I provided him with an incorrect answer he laughed out loud and said to me that I was an idiot and should not be in his class. I felt humiliated in front of my classmates.

Later, during a parent-teacher interview, he strongly recommended to my parents that I should not continue with my O Levels but move to the much easier Matriculation division. My parents and I had many a long discussion about this. Fortunately for me, they had enough faith in my abilities to continue to support my studies. I'm so glad that they did, because I made them proud with my final results.

Circumstances could have been very different if they had taken the Brother's advice.

I was not the only student that the Brother picked on. He seemed to pick on the more vulnerable, shy students (of which I was one) and take great pleasure in attempting to humiliate them in front of others.

Thinking back to those days, this Brother's attitude still makes me sad (rather than angry). How many students' lives did he change for the worse with his negative attitude? Contrast that with Sister Mary Francis. How many students benefited from her positive, uplifting and encouraging attitude? I hope many more benefited from her than were hurt by the Brother's attitude.

In our lives we will encounter many people with Sister Mary Francis's constructive attitude and others with the Brother's damaging attitude. I hope you are a positive person, because there is a whole lot of good that you can do by being optimistic.

Not only will you feel good about life but your positivity will rub off on others: your family, friends and all the people you come into contact with. People want to be around positive people. Positive people make others feel good and the energy can be electric.

'Optimism is the faith that leads to achievement. Nothing can be done without hope and confidence.'

HELEN KELLER

Attitude as a Speaker

Having a positive attitude as a speaker is paramount to how successful you are in preparing your message, building and finally delivering it. Negative thinking will impact the way you approach the speaking process and leave you feeling less confident and second-guessing yourself. This is not a good state to be in. Be positive in how you plan and build your message and you will be on a solid footing to deliver a strong speech.

POSITIVE ATTITUDE WHEN CONCEIVING YOUR MESSAGE

Being positive starts from the time you develop the message of your speech. You must believe that the message you create and deliver will provide good value for your audience. If negativity creeps in, stop for a moment and think about how you can turn it around so that you will provide value to the audience.

If you are still unsure, then confide in a trusted friend that you want to deliver a positive outcome for your audience and ask them how they can help you come up with ideas to make your message of more value.

Say you are preparing a speech on travel tips for your audience of baby boomers. Your mission is to provide information of value that will help your listeners to make their travel more enjoyable. Think from your audience's perspective.

What are the positive things that you can focus on that will help meet your goal? For people who are ageing, you may want to focus on health while on holiday, eating healthy food and avoiding food that may cause illness. Or you may focus on how they can maintain a daily regime of exercise or activities. You may consider how they can quickly overcome jet lag and start their holiday refreshed. Whatever you decide to include in your message, think positively that you can and will add value to your audience.

POSITIVE ATTITUDE WHEN PLANNING AND BUILDING YOUR MESSAGE

Planning and building a good speech takes time and requires effort. There may be frustrations along the way and time may be against you. In challenging moments, such as speaking within time restrictions, not having the right material for your message or not feeling that the speech has appropriate value, it is important that you keep positive. The right attitude will go a long way in keeping your spirits up and on track to do the right thing by your audience.

Let's go back to the example of preparing holiday tips for a speech for baby boomers. Consider that you want to provide them with a message in five parts that will help them have a better holiday. As is sometimes the case, let's say that you are running out of time to put your message together. What do you do? Think positively.

Can you make more time to make sure that you cover off the five parts? If so then fine, allocate more time to prepare your message. If this is not possible, keep thinking positive. Perhaps consider reducing the key parts to three parts. Sure it's a lower number and therefore reduced value, however if they are the best three of the original five, then your audience will still get great value from your message. Or is there another way to present your message? Perhaps you could add more illustration to help the audience assimilate your message quickly and easily.

Thinking positively will help you address challenges in a constructive way. There is always an answer. How we answer depends on our attitude. If you prepare and deliver your message in a positive way, success will come.

POSITIVE ATTITUDE WHEN DELIVERING YOUR MESSAGE

Delivering your message is show time. All the research, planning, building and practising is behind you. This is the moment of truth where all the hard work culminates in your performance.

The delivery phase is the undoing of many speakers as this is when negativity often creeps in. Just before most speakers present, they start to get nervous and negative self-talk begins.

This is where you as a speaker must have a positive attitude. If you have researched well, prepared your message appropriately and practised strongly, be assured that you will deliver a good speech. If you have done all of this then don't entertain any negative self-talk. Thinking positively just prior to and during delivery will help to put you in the right frame of mind to deliver your message.

An important point to note is that your focus should be on your message and not yourself. Think positively about how your message will provide good value.

POSITIVE ATTITUDE
FOLLOWING THE DELIVERY

After the delivery of your speech is also an important time to maintain a positive attitude. All the hard work has now been done, from preparing the speech to delivering it. Congratulations! What more do you need to do now?

Well, for you to enhance your message for future, this is a good time to assess what went well and what can be improved. As soon as their speech is complete, many speakers tend to focus on the negatives.

I forgot to cover a whole section.

The audience looked bored.

I should have used stronger body language.

I should have, I could have, I would have!

This reflection time is where it is imperative that a speaker maintains their positivity. Force yourself to think of all the good things you achieved during your speech.

The audience seemed to love the anecdote about my daughter's piggy bank savings.

They actively responded when I asked them about sharing their money-saving tips.

They gave me a resounding applause at the end.

So, first think of all the positives that you have achieved and feel proud of these achievements. Only after you feel good about all that went well should you allow yourself to reflect on how you can improve your speech for next time.

Speakers often receive feedback from audience members after the speech. This may be solicited or unsolicited. Sometimes the feedback is positive and it is a great feeling as a speaker to get commended.

Sometimes the feedback is negative. Your attitude will go far in terms of how you accept the feedback and apply it for future. If you take a defensive approach to receiving negative feedback then you may not learn from it. You are focusing inward and taking the feedback personally. However, if you are positive and receive the feedback with an outward-focused view, then you can automatically see how to improve your message for the future.

Summary

Like George the camp guide and Sister Mary Francis, we meet people every day who have a positive attitude. Having and maintaining a positive attitude in life is a good foundation to set you up for success.

This positive attitude also applies to you as a speaker. Keep the following points in mind during the various phases of your speech.

1. When conceiving your message, keep thinking of how you can add value to your audience. If you are unsure of the value, then discuss with a trusted friend who can provide honest feedback and positive suggestions.

2. Planning and building your message is a key phase that requires time and focus. It's easy to get distracted or frustrated, so maintaining a positive attitude will go a long way in keeping your spirits up and keep you on track to deliver good value for your audience.

3. It's show time when you deliver your message. It's also the time a speaker may feel vulnerable with negative thoughts creeping in. Stay positive by thinking about the value of your message rather than focusing on yourself.

4. Keep maintaining a positive attitude after the delivery of your message. Focus firstly on all the things that went well with your speech and feel proud of your achievements. Then reflect on what you can improve for next time. If you obtain negative feedback, consider it in a constructive manner by focusing on how it can help improve your message in the future.

CHAPTER 24

Be Inspirational

*'If your actions inspire others
to dream more, learn more, do more
and become more, you are a leader.*

JOHN QUINCY ADAMS

All great leaders inspire others in some way.

Martin Luther King was the great inspirational leader of the non-violent civil rights movement. King inspired millions of Americans, both black and white, to aspire to a more equal and just society.

Nelson Mandela campaigned for justice and freedom in South Africa. Mandela was jailed for 20 years for his opposition to apartheid. After release, he became the first president of democratic South Africa and helped heal the wounds of apartheid by his noble attitude to his former political enemies.

Mother Teresa is revered for living a life of poverty in the service the poor and destitute in India. Mother Teresa did this through her great compassion for others.

Inspirational people are not just famous people. There are

millions of ordinary people everywhere who are inspirational. Someone who inspires you could be your spouse, your friend, even your child.

This chapter will provide an understanding of what is required to become an inspirational speaker.

Let's review the three types of speakers who are inspirational:

- Optimistic people;

- Audacious people;

- Caring people.

As you read about each type of inspirational speaker bear in mind the following two important considerations:

- How you decide to brand yourself – you may choose to brand yourself as one of the three types of inspirational speakers or perhaps a combination of them;

- Customising the type of inspirational speaker you want to be for a particular speech by determining who your audience is, what the purpose of the presentation is and what your audience will be looking for from your message.

Optimistic People

Optimism and a positive attitude are brothers-in-arms. Like positive people, optimistic people are those who have a 'glass half full' mentality. They look at life in a positive light. Optimistic people look for opportunities, even when presented with challenges. They are energetic and spread their energy to others. They also give hope to others.

A good friend of mine, Ken Bernard, is the epitome of an optimistic person. Ken is at retirement age, however age is no barrier. Ken continues to work with tremendous enthusiasm and energy. Ken runs a number of self-help workshops and he is loved by workshop participants not only for his great subject-matter knowledge but also for the infectious energy he spreads to others. I have seen workshop participants light up with energy when Ken presents.

These same participants flock to speak to Ken after the workshops. That is a sign of an inspirational person; someone to whom people are drawn because they radiate so much energy.

HOW TO DEVELOP AN OPTIMISTIC ATTITUDE

I have read many inspirational books that have influenced my thinking on how to become more optimistic. Here's my take:

Decide to Become Optimistic

That's right; make a decision right now to be more optimistic. From this moment on, think positive. If someone annoys or irritates you, perhaps they are having a bad day. Simply bless them in your mind and think good things about them.

If you have a problem, think of the opportunities to turn that challenge into a positive. If you make a mistake, don't beat yourself up. Decide to learn from the mistake.

Action:

Challenge yourself to think positive for an entire day. On the nominated day (I'm hoping that it is today), challenge yourself to see everything in a positive light. Believe that all your experiences that day will be positive. Nothing will faze you. Every time you have a negative thought, zap it in your mind.

Attract Others

As soon as you start to think positively, you will radiate positive energy, begin to smile more and your energy will increase. Your body language changes for the better. This is where magic happens. You will notice people being drawn to you. They will be drawn to your smile. They will connect with your positive energy.

People don't want to be around negative people; they want to be charged up with positive people just like you are right now. Once you learn the magic of optimism and how people will be drawn to you, then you can use this to propel yourself and become an inspiration to others.

Action:

Decide that today will start differently. You will smile genuinely at people, even strangers, if they make eye contact with you. Say good morning in an energetic manner. Greet people with a glint in your eye. Feel good about yourself and make others feel good whenever the opportunity arises. Don't be disheartened if you do not get the response you thought, especially if not everybody smiles back at you. Keep positive and smile at the next person.

Keep going and soon you will begin to see the positive effect you have. Work colleagues will want to associate with you. Family and friends will begin to notice the positive attitude and newfound energy you bring and will want to be part of it. People will want to share in your enthusiasm and energy. And this all happened because one day you *decided* to have a more positive attitude.

INSPIRING WITH OPTIMISM AS A SPEAKER

People love speakers who are energetic and vibrant. Motivational speakers such as Anthony Robbins present with tremendous energy and enthusiasm. Can we all present like Anthony Robbins? No, we probably cannot and nor should we try to. Always be true to yourself; you can be an extrovert or an introvert and still present with more energy than you have previously done. Having an optimistic attitude is a decision only you can make. When you are preparing for your presentation, decide to be optimistic. Be optimistic that your material will bring *good value to your audience*. Be optimistic that you will conduct thorough research. Be optimistic that you will improve with each practice.

Be optimistic and present with energy and enthusiasm in front of your audience. Remain optimistic when answering questions that your audience asks you. Be optimistic when taking away learnings from your presentation to apply for future presentations.

Your optimism will start to *inspire others*; they will want to hear you more, be with you more and the ultimate compliment will be when they want to be optimistic … just like you. When that happens, you know that you are inspiring other people.

Audacious People

Audacious people are those who challenge the norm. They stand up for what they believe in. They don't give up even if their ideas are not popular. They believe that they can change things.

When most people think of inspirational people, often they nominate people who are audacious. People like Helen Keller ,who believed she could change things. And she did. Keller became deaf and blind before her second birthday. Despite this debilitating disability, she learned to read and write, and became the first deaf-blind person to gain a bachelor degree. She campaigned on issues of social welfare, women's suffering and rights for the disabled and she impressed many with her force of personality.

Another audacious person was Sir Winston Churchill. In 1940, Britain stood alone against the all-conquering Nazi war machine. After Hitler's troops had swept all before them, the invasion of Britain looked imminent. Churchill inspired the nation to fight on and achieve victory – whatever the cost. Five years later, British troops took part in the Allied landings in Normandy and over a year later completed the liberation of Europe. Churchill was an audacious leader who believed in what he stood for and inspired his forces to achieve victory against the tide.

HOW TO BECOME AN AUDACIOUS SPEAKER

If you want to inspire others by being audacious, *think* audaciously. Whatever your message may be, think outside the normal convention. Can you present a new concept around an old message? Can you make people think differently about your concept? Can you present in a way that has rarely been presented before?

Thinking audaciously and speaking in an audacious manner are two different things. Many of us can conjure things in our mind. We can be bold, courageous and outlandishly daring within the safe confines of our minds. Speaking audaciously is totally different. You need to have confidence, belief and courage that your audience will accept your trail-blazing ideas.

If you want to inspire by being bold, make sure you can

back up your material with real evidence and facts. People love courageous speakers with new concepts ... but only if those concepts are proven in some way. The best way to prove something is to provide evidence or even better to demonstrate it. If people can 'see' (literally or in their mind's eyes) then you have a much stronger chance of selling your concept to them.

Start small. Think of an idea that may not set the world on fire but something that may make a small difference in people's thinking. Think of the benefit it will have to your audience and present that to them.

A few years ago I joined a public speaking group that met fortnightly. Their meetings went for 2.5 hours between 7pm and 9:30pm. This made it a late evening for me as by the time I got home it was 10pm, and I had to work the next day. I made a recommendation to the club's board that we should make the meeting of one-hour duration. You should have seen their reaction!

'It won't work.'

'It's always been done this way.'

'Our members will not get enough practice time.'

I put my tail between my legs and walked away ... but only for a short while. I came back to them with an agenda that showed them how we could retain the most important speaking assignments and ensure that our members did not lose any practice time within a one-hour meeting. It took some convincing until I suggested we have a one-hour demonstration meeting that I would chair. They consented to this test session. At the end of the test session, I asked members if they still felt the one-hour session was too short for their practice. Most people agreed that the session was punchier than the existing 2.5-hour segment, without detracting from their practice time.

The board made a compromise to make the new sessions 1.5 hours. I was delighted. This gave all the members one hour back each meeting. And it was all because the *status quo* was challenged. This is a very minor example of making a difference. You too can start making a small difference around you if it will bring some benefit to yourself and others.

These small steps can then lead to bigger decisions, bolder actions, more courageous stances, and you can be seen as a person who stands by their convictions. As long as you are providing more and more value, people will look at you as an inspiration.

Action:

Start with small steps and learn from them to inspire bolder actions. Up the ante as you get more experience, take a few more risks and start to inspire others through courageous, audacious thoughts, ideas and actions.

Caring People

Caring people inspire others through their thoughtfulness and kindness. Pope Francis I, in my opinion, displays a certain humbleness with which he connects with the faithful, who are moved by his kindness and caring attitude. This Pope is inspiring by simply putting the laity first.

Action:

If you want to inspire others through caring and kindness, start today through small acts of kindness. Look for something nice to compliment someone about, and always be genuine. Look for opportunities to help someone do something better or provide them with ideas to improve – sharing your advice in a sensitive manner, of course.

HOW TO SPEAK AS A CARING PERSON

Chapter 16, Care for Your Audience, covered how to connect with others through your kindness and caring and here I will just add these important elements.

To inspire others with your presentation and display that you care about them, prepare your message with love. Yes, with love. They say that the best-cooked meals are ones that are prepared with love. It is the same with speeches.

Where can you find speeches filled with love? If you have ever heard a eulogy, then you will have heard a message filled with love. Eulogies are centered on the deceased person and it is with care and love that a message is prepared and delivered. Often included in eulogies are inspirational stories about the person (be it that they had a wonderfully positive attitude, or conquered their world with acts of courage or made the world a better place with their kindness).

To show yourself as a caring speaker, develop your message the same way you would prepare a eulogy.

Consider how you can put emotion into your message. This may mean preparing your message from you heart, adding emotional elements to it. Add personal stories so that your audience will remember you as a thoughtful and caring person.

Summary

To be an inspirational speaker, decide which kind of inspiration you want to be. This may be based on your particular audience and their expectations or how you want to portray yourself (your brand).

1. **To be an inspirational presenter through optimism:**

   • Decide to be optimistic;

   • Prepare your material to provide good value for your audience;

   • Do thorough research;

   • Practise your message and improve with each practice;

   • Present with energy and enthusiasm in front of your audience.

2. **To be an inspirational presenter by being audacious:**

   • Think audaciously, be different;

- Ensure you can back up your audacious message with facts and real content;

- Start small and learn from the experience;

- Be persistent, as audacious ideas (no matter how brilliant) will often be challenged;

- Keep going, up the ante, build your reputation as an audacious person.

3. **To be an inspirational presenter through caring:**

- Prepare your message with love and consideration;

- Prepare your message as if you were preparing for a eulogy, with respect;

- Add messages that will bring emotional responses from your audience;

- Add stories so that your audience will remember you as a thoughtful and caring person;

- Make caring for others your brand and give each message with all your heart.

Conclusion

Leave a Legacy

Dear Reader,

Many years ago, a work colleague of mine bragged about a grandfather who served with great distinction in the Australian army. Her grandfather was a decorated and well-known soldier and she was rightly very proud of his achievements.

I remember thinking of my own grandparents and sadly reflecting that there was nothing notable that future generations would remember of them. Sure, they were wonderful grandparents, and decent, honest, hardworking people whom I will remember for the rest of my life. But who else would remember them?

Not everyone can or wants to leave a legacy, but some of us will aim to have that as our mission. It is my hope that this book leaves a legacy, in helping you become a strong, confident speaker with messages that really connect. That's the legacy I want to leave.

How about *you*? What will people *remember* you for? What

will be the *value* you provide others? Will you provide value to a *handful* of people or *thousands*?

There is a wonderful business adage that says *'Count your success in people not profits'*.

Those who leave a legacy connect with others, touch lives and make a real difference. The difference could be to your customers, staff, family, community or even a nation. And some incredible people make a difference to the whole world.

Only you can decide the legacy you leave, to whom and to how many.

Why *waste* your *brilliant life*? Live it with love for yourself and love for others and leave a legacy that will be cast in stone.

Regards,

Mark

Acknowledgements

Zing! Speak like a Leader has been seven years in the making and I am proud of the end result. None of this would have been possible without the support of the following people.

Firstly to a work colleague, Simon Lenz, who was undertaking his own private project. Simon's disciplined approach and resilience inspired me to focus on the end goal of writing a book to help others. Simon served as a coach, meticulously checking each chapter and providing his forthright views. His philosophy of 'do your best work only' kept ringing in my ears as I progressed with the book, work and life. I am very grateful and appreciative of Simon for his friendship, guidance and support.

To the Captain Honey team, a massive thanks! Roz Hopkins project managed and edited *Zing! Speak Like A Leader* and did a brilliant job. Roz's thoughtful guidance, publishing wisdom and attention to detail are greatly appreciated.

Thanks to Bridget Blair who proofread the book with great diligence and careful consideration.

Thanks also to Natalie Winter for designing the cover with

the lion emerging from the shadow of a cat, cleverly illustrating how learned behaviours can fulfil dreams, in this case to be a leader.

Finally, to my wife Gayle without whose support I could not have completed this book. Allowing me the time to write and providing creative thoughts at just the right time pushed me to do my best work.

Mark D'Silva is founder and CEO of Speak 2 Peak.

After being a shy and introverted person for 30 years of his life, Mark made a decision to become a leader. His transformational journey commenced with seeking out great mentors, embarking on self-development programs and acquiring leadership skills. He progressed to managing complex change on multi-million dollar projects requiring exceptional communication skills.

Taking leadership positions in not-for-profit organisations and serving as president of a large community organisation and on the boards of entrepreneurial organisations helped Mark attain his aspirations of not just participating in life but actively leading.

As a speaker, Mark has won multiple Australian state public speaking titles and has represented Australia in the World Championship of Public Speaking finals held in Canada.

Through his business, Speak 2 Peak, Mark supports people who want to speak like leaders: with confidence, sincerity and passion.

Mark also appears as a guest speaker, delivering keynote speeches and master classes on strategies for building confidence, how to connect with people, and the leadership traits needed to become a successful leader.

www.ingramcontent.com/pod-product-compliance
Lightning Source LLC
Chambersburg PA
CBHW060338220326
41598CB00023B/2747